Praise for *The Firsts: Women Pilots and How they Changed the Airlines*

"This book of firsts is a MUST have for any aviation history enthusiast! Women with ordinary names like Emily and Bonnie, did the extraordinary! They came *FIRST* and opened opportunities for other women! Once their uniforms graced the flight deck, but as proof of their trailblazing, now hang in the Smithsonian Air and Space Museum for all to see. Their journeys were not easy, but led to an open door for others. Shipko even talks about the challenges of African-American women pilots and tells us the story of how ISA +21, Zonta, International and Sisters of the Skies were born, out of necessity and have endured, thriving as models of sisterhood and support. Shipko not only tells the story of U.S. women, but she also takes us around the globe of *FIRSTS* from Norway, to Australia, India, Kenya, Nigeria, China and Japan."

Carole Hopson
Author of A Pair of Wings,
A Novel Inspired by Pioneer Aviatrix Bessie Coleman

"The ambitious and brave women described in this informative and inspiring book laid the groundwork for today's aspiring female pilots. As Emily Warner, first woman hired to fly for an airline (Frontier) and also the first to achieve the rank of Captain (in 1976), once said, 'Individually we are grains of sand; together we become a beach.'"

CDR Marie Ernst USNR (Ret.)

"As I read *The Firsts: Women Pilots and How They Changed the Airlines* I was fascinated as Mary Shipko told the stories of so many women from all over the globe who made their dreams to fly a reality against so many hurdles placed before them because they were female. She tells their well-researched stories, as well as her own, while interweaving the historic laws, acts, and safety developments that eventually led to the elimination of discrimination and harassment in the workplace. The organization of the book is especially interesting as it also provides selected commentary, poetry, and photos and descriptions of the planes these ladies flew. I would encourage any young woman who is considering a career as a pilot to read this book. In fact, it is a good read for any woman looking to enter a career once dominated by men."

Noel Priseler, Co-founder and Organizer,
Book and Breakfast Club, 20 years strong

"Be ready to read this book from start to finish! I could not set down *The Firsts: Women Pilots and How they Changed the Airlines.* I constantly wanted to know the women's stories and where they ended up. I felt like I was face-to-face with these incredible pilots and listening to their journeys. As an Airline Transport Pilot and an Assistant Professor of Practice in Commercial Aviation, I learned so much about this depreciated history. Even today, I can relate to the 'modern cowboy' and others being warned of 'a woman in the cockpit.' Sexism can still be found in flight training and professional environments. I always recommend that future and current aviators find a mentor because of the stigma of women pilots. This book has amazing information to let women know that they are not alone. The 99's, ISA+21, and Women in Aviation International are invaluable resources. Awareness, education, and perseverance will trail-blaze future generations of women of all nationalities in aerospace. These pioneers' stories are inspirational to any reader. I am proud to be a part of the 'Next' generation. Thank you, Mrs. Mary Shipko for bringing light to *The Firsts.*"

Rebecca Parker, Airline Transport
Pilot Assistant Professor of Practice of
Commercial Aviation, Delta State University

"This is the story by an insider of what several of the early women pilots for commercial airlines faced—the good and the bad, the irritating and the fun, the friendly and the hostile, the depressing and the inspiring, including the growing efforts by the early pilots to mentor those that followed them and be mentored themselves by other women. Mary Shipko tells a seldom told story of an important chapter in the history of aviation and the history of women in the workplace."

Bonnie Tiburzi, author of *Takeoff! The Story of America'sFirst Woman Pilot for a Major Airline.*

THE FIRSTS

Women Pilots and How they Changed the Airlines

Mary Bush Shipko

The Firsts:
Women Pilots and How they Changed the Airlines

Copyright © 2023 by Mary Bush Shipko

ISBN 979-8-9859509-4-6

Dedicated to the men & women of
Women In Aviation, Experimental Aircraft
Association, and International Society
of Women Airline Pilots.

Your support and encouragement
helped me make this book possible.
You made a difference in my life.

CONTENTS

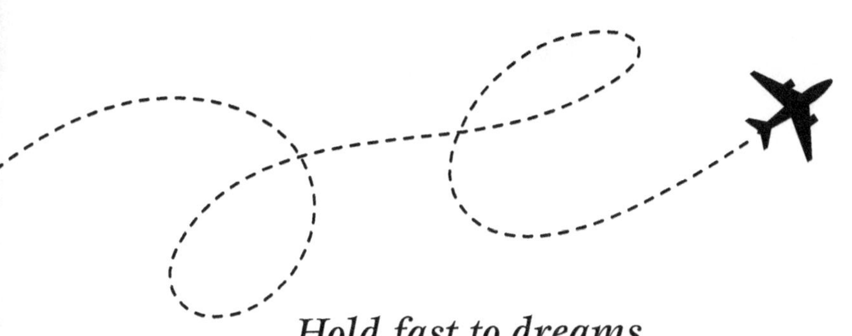

Hold fast to dreams
For if dreams die
Life is a broken-winged bird
That cannot fly.

Langston Hughes

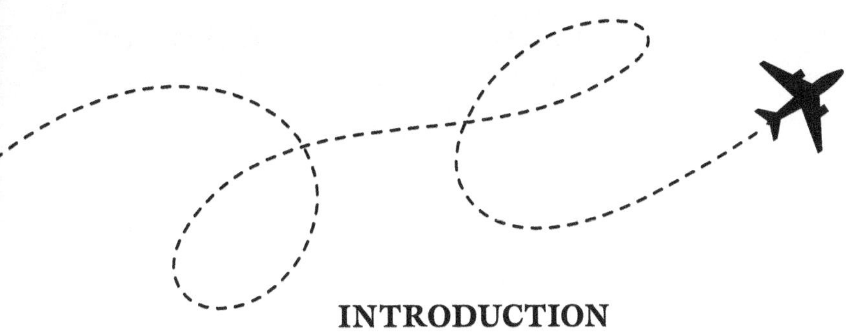

"If a Man Can Do It, a Woman Can, Too."

AS THE NEW aviation industry grew, women wanted to be part of it. In particular, Amelia Earhart, a bold and brave American aviation pioneer, wanted several things. She wanted women to be considered equal to men. She wanted to fly. And she wanted Americans to use airplanes as a form of public transportation. Amelia Earhart helped create a world in which such things were possible. As such, she was an important woman in American history, making valuable contributions that still affect the world today.

The aviation industry—the business of flying airplanes—began in the early 1900s, at a time when it was normal for women's lives to be restricted. Men in the aviation industry regulated what women could and could not do.

For example, women could not take formal flying lessons, or fly in the military or for the airlines. Women could, however, fly their own plane or someone else's to women's events, air races, and fly-ins. Women pilots could also set flight records. Louise Thaden, who learned to fly in 1928, set several records and encouraged other women to do the same. She wanted American women to hold as many flying records as they could.

One record many women wanted to set was flying across the Atlantic Ocean. In 1927, American aviator Charles Lindbergh did just that and was able to claim the Orteig Prize, a reward that New York hotel owner Raymond Orteig was offering to the first aviator to make a nonstop flight across the Atlantic. After that historic flight, many women said, "If a man can do it, a woman can, too."

Amelia Earhart was recruited to do just that. She agreed to fly for free, and to write a book about the flight. She knew it was high-risk. Until Lindbergh's success, many pilots had tried and failed, crashing on land or ditching into the sea. Some had even lost their lives. Earhart wrote the poem "Courage" in 1927 before anyone had even asked her about crossing the Atlantic. She clearly recognized that courage was essential for big change because she wrote: "Courage is the price that Life exacts for granting peace." (See Appendix B for Earhart's full poem.)

Women pilots in the 1920s and 1930s were routinely made fun of, or demeaned, in public. For example, the Women's Air Derby, created in 1929 as the first official women's-only air race, was called the "Powder Puff Derby," a name meant to devalue the race and its impact. During the research for his bestselling book *Fly Girls*, Keith O'Brien found "that sexism was blatant—and everywhere. Male pilots belittled [the women]. The press often disparaged them too." Women flying for any reason was frowned upon. The general belief of the time was that women should be at home taking care of their families. In response to that attitude, women pilots formed an organization specifically for offering support to other female pilots. The organization was called the Ninety-Nines and was formed in 1929. It is still an active organization today.

As the aviation industry developed, extending to the military and eventually the airlines, women would be left behind. While no laws specifically banned women from the airline cockpit in 1914, they would be excluded nonetheless. Simply put, women were not welcome in the aviation industry.

Amelia Earhart tried to change that. As a public figure, she helped with the development of major U.S. airlines such as Trans World Airways (TWA) and Northeastern Airlines. She tried to convince airlines to hire women pilots. In 1934, she hoped things were changing for the better when Central Airlines hired female pilot Helen Richey. However, Helen was not allowed to become a permanent employee, and had to leave.

By 1940, World War II was brewing. Europe was already at war, and some American women pilots went to England to fly for the military there. Back home, inspired by Earhart, women pilots pushed to fly for the U.S. military. After much negotiating, the women pilots were allowed to volunteer as pilots. The organization called Women Airforce Service Pilots (WASP) was formed in 1942. Not until 1993 were women allowed to fly combat aircraft.

Assisting with the war effort, the WASP women flew from 1942 to 1944. They delivered planes from the factory to the men in the field and performed other domestic flying tasks as needed. Many people did not like that these women were doing a "man's job," and they complained—loudly—that the women were taking jobs away from men.

The women pilots were treated badly. Sometimes they were given undesirable planes, and other times they were evaluated unfairly, meaning that some people refused to acknowledge the women's abilities at all. Negative articles in newspapers criticized the women pilots. The WASP program ended when the military said they no longer needed the women. The women left the military service well qualified to fly commercially, and some would apply to the airlines. But before they could be hired, a new law by the U.S. Commerce Department would keep them out of the commercial flying industry for the next twenty years.

Still following in Amelia Earhart's footsteps, though, many women pushed for changes that would allow them to be airline pilots. During the 1960s, when strides toward gender equality were being made in other aspects of life, women pilots saw their chance. This book introduces you to some of the very first women airline pilots to break through that long-held gender barrier, as well as major laws and developments that make the airline cockpit a friendly place today.

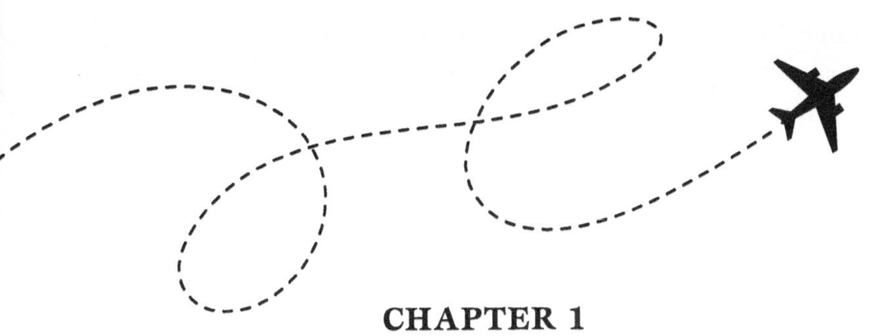

<h1 align="center">CHAPTER 1</h1>

<h1 align="center">Emily Warner</h1>

EMILY'S HEART POUNDED as she spun around on the runway just after landing at Stapleton International Airport in Denver. She was flying a single-engine Cessna 140, a tail dragger that was prone to weathervaning, meaning that it would often spin freely in the wind when on the ground. It was only her third solo flight, and as the airplane rotated by itself, Emily worried that her flying days were already over. She had been warned that the plane could spin if the wind caught it, but she had not taken proper care to avoid it. She was upset with herself. She would have to pay attention to every detail in the future. Emily had just learned a valuable lesson. She would become very safety minded.

Emily Warner was an Irish-American beauty with a winning smile. She was born in 1939 in Denver, Colorado, to a working-class family of seven; she had three older brothers and a twin sister. Her father worked for the railroad and didn't make much money; he often had trouble trying to support their large family. To Emily's embarrassment, they often qualified for programs or services for poor families such as free or discounted summer camp. Sometimes during holidays Emily's father was lucky enough to receive free train tickets so that the family could visit relatives in Minnesota. Emily developed her love of traveling and seeing new things on those family holiday trips. Emily's mother was a singer who encouraged Emily to learn new things. For example, at her mother's urging, Emily took classes in poise and modeling. Emily was not afraid to take risks. In fact, she got her first job after a classmate dared her to apply for it.

Emily had never thought about being a pilot, but she also knew that she did not want to remain poor. Her mother made her dresses out of chicken feed sacks because it was all they could afford, and Emily had often been humiliated by classmates and neighborhood kids because of that. She wanted to wear regular clothes made of regular fabric.

Emily experienced three events in high school that affected her thoughts of her future.

First, her class visited a women's college and learned about different careers for women. It was the 1950s, and up to that point, Emily had not realized that women could have careers the way her dad had. She was just starting to understand that women could be independent and support themselves. She began to see a different reality for herself.

Second, she read *Wind, Sand and Stars* by Antoine de Saint-Exupéry, a book that introduced her to the magic of flight. Within the book, Saint-Exupéry took Emily aloft on his flights. She felt his bravery and love of flying and was in awe of the risks he had taken. She became intrigued by the idea of flying, but it was merely a fantasy. She still never imagined that she could one day fly herself.

The third significant happening was when her classmate dared her to apply for a job at a local store. Emily took the dare because she thought about the money she could earn; the memory of those chicken-feed sack dresses she had worn when she was young was still fresh in her mind. With a job, she would be able to buy her own clothes—*new* clothes. She got the job, and after a short time at that store, she changed jobs to work at a department store, which was much larger. She worked as a sales clerk and regularly met airline stewardesses who came in to buy clothes and other items. Recalling Saint-Exupéry's adventures, Emily pictured herself in an airplane. She dreamt of becoming a stewardess since she thought that was the closest she could come to flying. Nowadays airline stewardesses are called flight attendants.

After graduating from high school, Emily worked full-time at her sales clerk job, but she kept dreaming about becoming a stewardess. She imagined what it would be like to ride in a plane.

Emily's supervisor knew Emily wanted to be a stewardess, and one day she invited Emily to a special dance at her daughter's college. Emily would have to fly to get there. It would be the first time Emily ever rode in a plane. "It will give you the opportunity to see what a stewardess does," her supervisor said. Her supervisor considered a stewardess job to be too unconventional and hoped Emily would decide she didn't want to be one after all once she saw what a stewardess did. Indeed, Emily decided not to become a stewardess, but not because of seeing them in action. It was because of something else from that trip.

Recalling passages from *Wind, Sand and Stars*, Emily asked if she could sit in the cockpit of the plane on the way home. This wasn't too unusual in those days, especially for smaller planes, and she was allowed. As she quietly watched the pilots perform their duties, Emily thought, "Wow, the pilots have the best job!"

After the flight, she spoke to the copilot about the wonder and awe she had experienced as they flew.

"Maybe you should take flying lessons," he said.

This surprised Emily. A woman could take flying lessons? The next day, Emily called Clinton Aviation and Flight School, at Stapleton Airport in Denver, to see if it was true.

It *was* true—a woman *could* take flying lessons!

Emily started taking lessons the following week. The year was 1958.

- - - - - -

Emily took a bus to her first lesson. It was snowing in Denver, and the weather was too bad to fly during that first lesson. So, instead, Emily learned how to do a walk-around, a necessary activity before any flight. She learned the use of checklists, too, as part of the walk-around. Checklists help a pilot know that they haven't missed anything; they help them check that the plane is ready for flight. Then, Emily and her flight instructor taxied around the airport in an airplane for the rest of the lesson. When the instructor asked her to press down on the plane pedals just like she would in a car, Emily commented that she didn't drive. The instructor said, "Good—no bad habits to break."

Each week on her day off from her sales clerk job, Emily took the bus out to the airport for a lesson. She was having fun, so much so that her flight instructor had to speak to her.

"Listen," he said, "you're going to have to really buckle down if you want to fly. Flying is serious and requires lots of study and dedication. It's not just about having fun."

So Emily buckled down and studied hard. In fact, she became a very dedicated student.

And each week, Emily worked hard at the department store, too, saving to pay for that week's flight lessons. The lessons were always the highlight of her week.

- - - - - -

Emily had been taking lessons for a few months when she learned that they needed a secretary at the flight school. She applied for the job, deciding to leave her job as a sales clerk. However, her supervisor at the department store begged Emily to stay, even offering her a promotion. She told Emily that there was no future in flying for a girl.

"You're making a big mistake," the supervisor said.

Emily saw it differently though.

Working at the airport gave her the opportunity to fly more often and helped her gain more experience as a pilot. Emily especially loved flying over the Rocky Mountains. She loved to look down at the mountain peaks as she flew. It made her feel both big and small. The world was so beautiful, and the future so open; Emily felt so free!

Emily loved everything about Clinton Aviation and Flight School. She loved the employees, the planes, the hangar that housed the planes, the smells of oil and gas, the noises, and the friendships she developed.

Emily had been welcomed at the flight school first as a student and now as a secretary. She was young and friendly and, even though she was a female, she was not viewed as a threat, as someone who would take a so-called "male" job. As such, the men pilots treated her well, supporting her flying endeavors. She eventually became an instructor at the school herself, teaching others to fly. Some students refused to have a women instructor; those who complained were given a male instructor.

In the late 1960s, as part of her work at Clinton Aviation and Flight School, Emily starred in a Federal Aviation Administration (FAA) safety video about how to fly safely in the mountains since there were many accidents related to mountain flying. Topics covered in the video included foehn winds, density altitude and turbulence, and other concerns. Foehn winds result when the weather is different on one side of the mountain than the other, such as rain on the windward side and heat and dryness on the leeside, as is typical in Denver. Thirty-knot winds on the windward side become sixty-knot winds on the leeward side. Pilots need to be aware of this condition so that they can fly safely.

As a flight instructor, Emily taught men who then went on to become airline pilots, working for large commercial companies and flying planes full of people. This seemed unfair to Emily; she wanted to be an airline pilot, too. Flying small planes and teaching others was great, but she wanted more. She wanted to go all in; instead of just dipping her toe in the water, she wanted to swim.

In 1967, when she was twenty-eight years old, Emily applied for a pilot job at Frontier Airlines. The airline, however, said they'd *never* hire a woman. Emily asked the chief pilot what she needed to do to change their minds. The chief pilot said, "Well, for starters, get an Airline Transport Pilot rating, and get some flight time in multi-engine airplanes. But I still doubt any airline will hire a woman." An Airline Transport Pilot rating, or ATP rating, is a certificate required for pilots who want to fly as an airline captain.

Emily knew from news articles that a Black pilot, Marlon Green, had been hired by Continental Airlines in 1963, but that it had been a long process. The airlines didn't want to hire him because he was Black, so he had to take the airlines all the way to the Supreme Court. As a woman, Emily faced a similar challenge. She knew she was a skilled pilot and knew she was better qualified than many of her male students who had already become airline pilots at commercial companies. At the same time, though, she wasn't prepared to go all the way to the Supreme Court just to get hired! She hoped, instead, to be readily welcomed into the ranks.

The next year, 1968, Emily read a newspaper clipping about Turi Wideroe, who had been hired by Scandinavian Airlines. Turi had been the first female pilot hired by a major airline in the western world. Encouraged by this news, Emily applied to all three airlines that were based in Denver: Frontier (for the second time), Continental, and United. She felt that Frontier was her best chance since it was her hometown airline, having started operations in Denver in 1950.

Emily hoped her flying licenses and experience would qualify her to be an airline pilot. She yearned to be the first female airline pilot in the United States. Would she be?

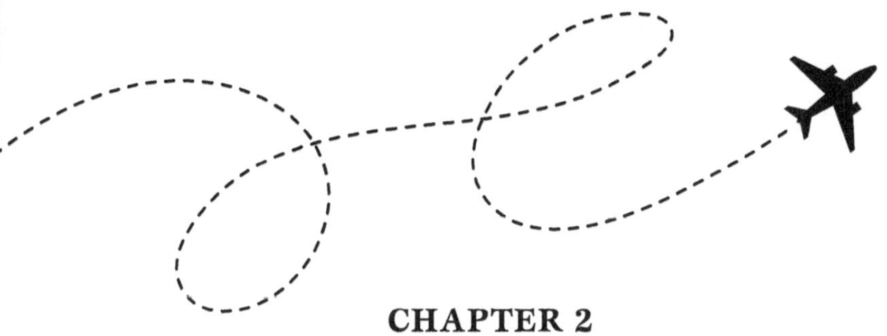

CHAPTER 2

Bonnie Tiburzi

BONNIE TIED DOWN her airplane as dark clouds rolled in and wind whipped around her; she had just outrun an unexpected storm. With the storm approaching, she had abandoned her flight path, making a U-turn and landing at the first airport she saw. Now, as she closed up her single-engine Cessna, the airport operator walked across the ramp to greet her.

"Are you Bonnie?" he asked.

How did he know her name? Had she done something wrong?

"Your dad's on the phone," he said.

Bonnie's dad was a retired airline pilot, and Bonnie knew that he would know how to locate her. He had been following the impending storm and Bonnie's flight plan and hadn't wasted any time in tracking her down to check if she was safe. No telling how many airports he had called before he found her.

Bonnie Tiburzi was a young East Coast woman who had been born about ten years after Emily Warner in Danbury,

Connecticut, in 1948. She had never heard of Emily. Bonnie had large brown eyes and lovely dark hair that hung down her back. For her, becoming an airline pilot was an early life decision, as both her father and brother were airline pilots. Her dad had eventually left the airlines to start a flight school and charter company that flew from Danbury to New York City. While growing up, Bonnie spent a lot of time at her father's company, which was called a fixed-base operation.

When she was in her teens, Bonnie and her family moved to Pompano, Florida, where she attended high school. When she told her high school guidance counselor that she wanted to be an airline pilot, she was told to pick a more realistic goal. Bonnie asked, "Why can't I be an airline pilot?" The counselor told her that there were no women airline pilots and that she would grow up to be nothing unless she picked a more realistic goal like teaching or nursing.

Bonnie received her basic training and flight licenses from Pompano Aviation at the Pompano Air Park. She first flew by herself, called soloing, in 1969 at the age of twenty-one. She continued to fly and soon passed her private pilot's rating. As she advanced in her flight ratings, the owner of Pompano Aviation took her under his wing, helping her to build flight time by giving her opportunities such as delivering a plane or being a copilot on larger planes. Building flight time is important because pilots generally have to have flown a certain number of hours to advance in their careers. After Bonnie received her instructor certificate, the owner then hired her to teach others. Bonnie also built flight time by flying charters, which are unscheduled flights, and making occasional ferry trips. The Bahamas off the coast of Florida was a popular destination. Some of the Bahamian islands are very close in size with Bimini, a district of the Bahamas, covering around sixty miles. Two casinos, one in Freeport, Grand Bahama, and the other in Nassau, were popular destinations for gamblers, people who liked to bet money. The gamblers would fly over to the island casinos for the evening in charter flights, and Bonnie would fly them home afterward, usually in the wee hours of the morning and often after they had lost their money.

Bonnie kept building her flight time in hopes of one day getting a job as an airline pilot. By this time, her brother had already become an airline pilot. When she asked him about her chances, he told her that airline jobs were saved for men with families. It was this mindset as well as the scarcity of airline jobs that continued to keep women out of the commercial airline profession.

However, in the fall of 1972, while visiting her sister in New York City, Bonnie was offered a special opportunity. She met the editor of *Harper's Bazaar*. He told her the magazine was planning a Florida feature article and invited her to be included in the article. Bonnie was ecstatic at the chance to be in the magazine. A journalist came to Florida and interviewed Bonnie about her desire to be an airline pilot and took photographs of her and the planes she flew. The magazine article was due out in January 1973. Bonnie was very excited to be in *Harper's Bazaar* and hoped the article would help her in her quest to get a job as an airline pilot. There were still no women airline pilots in the United States. Bonnie hoped she would be the first. Would she be?

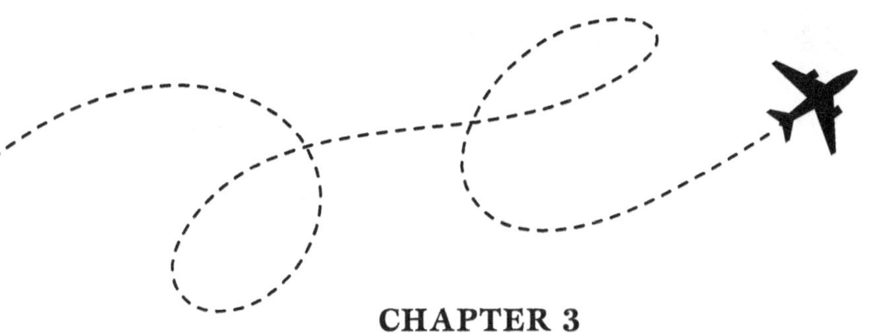

CHAPTER 3

Mary Bush

MARY WAS CONCERNED as the compass spun wildly. She hoped it would stop spinning and correct itself. She needed it in order to fly back to Florida from the Bahamas. A compass was all she had to help guide her until the Fort Lauderdale VOR, a radio-range navigation system for pilots, would start working. Mary was determined to just maintain her heading, or direction, until the compass settled down. Usually she could see the Florida coastline by now, but low visibility was obscuring it. She was flying through the Devil's Triangle, which is also known as the Bermuda Triangle, where ships and airplanes were rumored to have disappeared. Was that the reason the compass was acting so crazy? She wasn't sure she believed in the mystery of the Devil's Triangle, but at the same time, she had known of planes that had disappeared in the triangle, even in clear skies and good weather. She tried to dismiss the thought.

Mary Bush, a quintessential beauty with blonde hair and blue eyes, was born into an aviation family in Fort Lauderdale, Florida, in 1949. In high school, she started taking flying lessons from her pilot father. By the time she graduated, her family had fallen on hard times financially, so she started working right after graduation. While working part-time, Mary progressed in her flight ratings, hoping to get a paying flying job. She also attended Miami Dade Junior College part-time.

In 1969, Mary signed up for golf as her required physical education (PE) class at college. However, when she showed up for class, the instructor refused to let her stay, saying, "Golf is not a woman's sport." Mary left the class and took gymnastics instead. In 1969, society still expected traditionally defined gender roles. Certain activities were for men; certain activities were for women. It wasn't just society either. Mary's mother wanted her to get married and have children. While Mary wanted that too, she wanted to be an airline pilot first. She loved flying and wanted to make a living from it; she wanted to fly people from place to place.

Mary soon completed her commercial flight rating, a certificate based on the number of hours of flight time a pilot has logged, and began to earn money as a pilot flying cargo. Cargo is another word for shipments of goods. There were many small operators who delivered cargo all over the Bahamas and the Caribbean Basin in the 1960s and 1970s. World War II aircraft like the Douglas DC-6 and C-46 were cheap planes for operators to use, so they were popular among these companies. She wasn't flying people around as she still hoped to someday do as an airline pilot, but it was still exciting for Mary to fly these large transport aircraft and to visit many countries and islands that she had never been to before.

There are usually two pilots in a plane at a time. Many of the pilots for these planes that delivered cargo did not want to fly with a woman, so the work was not very steady. Mary was thankful, though, that there were always one or two pilots that would fly with her as the copilot. Mary was good at handling emergencies, so she began to gain a good reputation as a pilot, changing some pilots' minds about flying with her.

Growing up, Mary was often told by her brothers and the men around the airport that women were not as smart as men. They would say, "Women should not compete with men." And, more specifically, they would say to Mary, "*You* should not compete with men." Hearing such things was hard for Mary. She often felt frustrated. But it also motivated her. She would think to herself, "I will show them." As time went on, she would also go to church and pray for God's guidance.

The navigation aids for flying around the Bahamas and the Caribbean were very primitive; they weren't sophisticated like today's aids. *To navigate* means to find one's way, to have some direction. Nowadays people have "navigators" on their phones or in their cars that tell them where to turn, but in the 1960s and 1970s, pilots did not have such navigational aids. Pilots used what was called "dead reckoning" to find their way. This meant that they relied only on a compass heading, speed, and the time flown in order to successfully reach their destination.

- - - - - -

Mary received extensive training and experience on a plane called the Beechcraft D-18. The Beechcraft D-18 looks very much like the twin-engine Lockheed plane that Amelia Earhart flew on her last flight. After the war, D-18 planes were plentiful, making them popular with small freight and charter companies. These were often the planes that Mary flew to the Bahamas. While gaining experience in this aircraft, Mary had brakes fail, tires blow out upon landing, and engine failures. For example, on one landing, Mary applied the brakes only to find that the pedals went all the way down to the floor, which generally means that the brakes are failing. She pumped the brakes madly but could not revive them. It was a scary situation. Can you imagine being in a large vehicle and not being able to stop? Luckily, though, Mary was landing in Fort Lauderdale, where the runway was wide and long. Having a wide and long runway allowed her to roll the plane to a stop. Then, she asked to be towed off the runway.

Another time, on the way over to Andros Island in the Bahamas, the temperature of Mary's right engine had started to climb, so she shut the engine down, proceeded to the airport, and made a one-engine landing. As a result of these kinds of experiences, Mary became very skilled in thinking fast and was able to handle flying emergencies with ease.

- - - - - - -

Mary earned her commercial flying license in the D-18 and then went looking for work. Every day at sunrise, she rode around the Fort Lauderdale and Miami airports in her old VW bug wearing the universal pilot's uniform, a white shirt and black pants; she had her flight bag in the back seat of her car. Most days no one was interested in a woman pilot, but one day her luck changed. The owner of a small cargo company needed a last-minute pilot. His first officer, another name for the copilot, had not shown up for work and the flight needed to depart on time in order to keep on schedule. Mary was hired, and soon she found herself sitting in the right seat of the four-engine DC-6 heading down to an island in the Caribbean.

The twin-engine Curtis C-46 was another WWII aircraft popular with freight companies. Mary started flying it with a guy named Starvin' Marvin, who flew vegetables from the Bahamas to the states. Mary and Marvin transported cucumbers, squash, and tomatoes. Mary received her C-46 type rating, one of very few women to hold this rating, or license. Having a rating on the C-46 meant that she could fly as captain, or head pilot, on that particular airplane, instead of being the copilot, or first officer.

Mary also flew building supplies over to the Bahamas. On one flight early in the morning, they were carrying a load of lumber. The lumber had been checked in and weighed the day before but had sat on the ramp all night. As luck would have it, it had rained all night. The next morning, the lumber was loaded and they headed for Nassau. On takeoff, though, the airplane would not leave the ground. A long runway and excessive speed were needed to finally break ground. The plane still barely flew. The rain the night before had doubled the weight of the lumber. The flight over was slow with the heavy load, but they managed to land in Nassau without incident.

On another flight, a starry, moonless night flying out of Miami International on a DC-7, the flight engineer had failed to extend the flaps when requested during pre-flight takeoff. A DC-7 will not fly without flaps if it's heavily loaded right after takeoff. With great care, Mary finessed the old plane to something in between flying and stalling until they had gained a little bit of altitude. No doubt they had all cheated death simply because Miami Beach had mostly one-story buildings in 1973, which allowed them to stagger out at low altitude.

After that incident, with Mary's show of bravery and skill, many more men pilots were willing to fly with her.

Another plane, the DC-3, was the workhorse of World War II, meaning that it was dependable and durable. It was also a workhorse for many small cargo companies. Mary flew copilot on flights to the Diamond salt ponds on Long Island in the Bahamas, carrying supplies and workers. She also carried the *Miami Herald* to Nassau and food and supplies for the general store to Great Harbor.

Upon seeing an ad in the *Miami Herald* for pilots, Mary answered it. The United States Coast Guard was looking for pilots. She was told, however, that they did not hire women pilots. It was 1973. The world was changing, but not fast enough. Disappointed but determined, Mary continued on, flying charter planes and cargo.

In November of 1974, she received her airline transport rating in the DC-3, earning her type rating at the same time. This is the highest certification a pilot can earn. It represents extensive work and preparation and is important for pilots who wish to make a lifelong career of aviation. Type ratings are required for flying large aircraft, and additional training is needed for each specific aircraft. All mail that Mary received related to aviation was addressed to Mark, the *y* of her name having been changed to a *k*, because surely it must be a boy earning all these licenses.

In 1974, on a trip from Fort Lauderdale to Norman's Cay, Mary almost ran out of runway. Norman's Cay is the first island in the Exuma chain of islands in the Bahamas. The chain is famous for its sapphire-blue waters, the most beautiful water in the world. From the air, the islands look like little jewels surrounded by sparkling water of varying hues of aqua, blue, and green.

On approach, the windsock was dead, indicating little to no wind, but there was a slight tailwind. Mary didn't touch down right at the edge of the runway, which is something she would later learn to do in order to allow more space. The runway at Norman's Cay is bordered by water on three sides. Mary stood on the brakes and finally stopped just fifty feet before the water. She had often heard the phrase, "The runway behind you is of no use," and that ran through her head all night. In the morning, she surveyed the little airport and vowed to be more observant in the future. Pilots must always be paying attention to their surroundings.

While Mary enjoyed all of these adventures flying cargo, she still dreamt of flying passengers, of working for an airline. Flying for an airline was the pinnacle of a pilot's career—the opportunity many pilots strived for. To Mary, being a woman, it seemed like an impossible dream, but she was determined to try. Would it be her? Would she become the first female airline pilot in the United States?

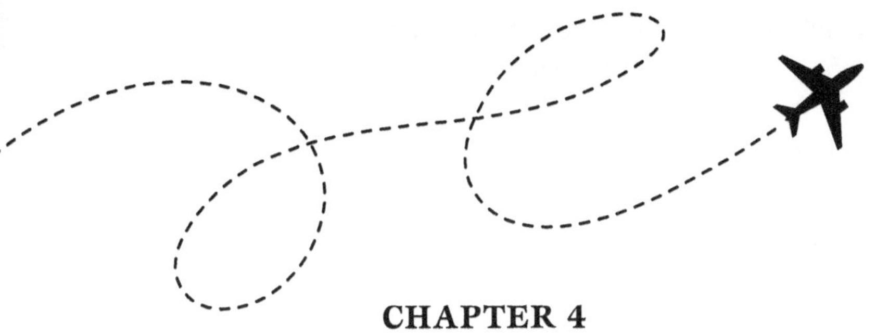

CHAPTER 4

Norah O'Neill

THE FURTHEST YOU could be from Miami, Florida, and still be in the United States was where Norah O'Neill was learning to fly: Alaska. From a military family with roots in Seattle, Washington, Norah fell in love with flying on a short flight from Talkeetna, Alaska, to a Mount Denali glacier. She was twenty-three and had accepted a modeling job for a photo shoot on the glacier. Pilot Don Sheldon, flying a single-engine plane on skis, had deposited the magazine crew and models on the mountain. Norah was struck by the incredible beauty she saw from the air; she liked the way her cares seemed to stay on the ground while she was not. When Don returned to pick the crew and models up, Norah asked him what it took to learn to fly. Trying to discourage her, he said, "It takes lots of time, work, money, and dedication." But that didn't discourage her. Within a month, Norah had earned a private license.

In 1967, while she was in high school, Norah was told she could be a teacher, nurse, or a secretary. But Norah said, "I don't want to be any of those things. Why do boys get the best jobs?" She was determined to do something exciting.

She earned her basic flight licenses in Alaska. These basic licenses allowed her to fly certain types of planes, but she couldn't yet transport people or cargo. The licenses allowed her to build flight time only, which limited her; she couldn't make money from flying yet. When winter set in, she went back to her parents, who were then living in San Diego, California. In San Diego, she continued working on her flight ratings, completing her commercial rating. In the spring, she went back to Alaska and earned her instructor's rating in Anchorage, Alaska. An instructor's rating is a certificate that would allow her to teach others to fly. Now she could start to earn a living at flying.

Except it wasn't so simple. No one would hire her as an instructor. It was 1973, and no flight centers in Anchorage needed any *women* flight instructors. However, as luck would have it, Norah knew the owner of a flying service and flight school in Fairbanks, Alaska. She gave him a call. He hired her, thinking that there might be a lot of servicemen from the nearby Air Force base that wanted to learn to fly and who would be delighted to learn from a pretty young woman. The owner thought it would give his school a competitive edge—an advantage. It turned out that he was right. Norah, indeed, was a popular instructor, teaching both the servicemen and their wives how to fly.

However, the other instructors did not like that there was a female instructor. Maybe it was jealously, or maybe it was fear that Norah's teaching would be inferior to that of a male. The chief pilot actually quit because of Norah. He stated that he would not work for a company with a woman pilot instructor because he believed that a female teaching people to fly would result in airplane accidents, and he wanted no part of it. In today's world, his reasoning sounds flawed. It *is* flawed. It is like saying that a woman cannot teach math and if she does, the result will be a lot of mathematical errors. In reality, it doesn't matter what someone's gender is; what matters is their competence and skill. Norah had both competence and skill. Additionally, she had enthusiasm and self-motivation. She was determined!

Most people can relate to the loneliness of being left out of a group, especially when you are trying so hard to fit in. These attitudes from the men pilots kept Norah from something she wanted: to belong. She wanted to be part of the group of instructors; she wanted to hang out with them at the end of the day and exchange stories, jokes, or new teaching ideas. But the men didn't want to include her—and it was all because she was a woman. There was no other reason.

Norah persevered, though, and kept working there; by Christmas 1974, she had been working as a flying teacher for nine months. She felt as though people were warming up to her, starting to appreciate her. Most of the staff and pilots at the school were friendly to her even if they didn't include her in their "clique." She decided to throw a Christmas party. She thought it would be a great way to gain everyone's acceptance; she invited everyone at the flight school.

No one came to Norah's party. It hurt her deeply.

With the realization that her colleagues really did not like her or want her working there, Norah thought about what to do. She decided to stay at the job. The flying was good, after all, and she thoroughly enjoyed the work. Maybe with more time, the others would come to appreciate and accept her for who she was and what she was able to do. Until then, though, she kept her head high and focused on her job and her passion for flying.

In addition to teaching, Norah flew charters to rural communities, and she also flew up and down the pipeline, which was under construction. The pipeline system is an oil transportation system in Alaska.

Few roads go north from Fairbanks. As such, most communities in northern Alaska have to be reached by air. So, Norah flew passengers in and out of these communities. However, many of the passengers were horrified to see a woman pilot and would tell her so. While it was often disheartening for Norah, she tried to see it through their eyes. Change is difficult for most people, and it can be especially difficult in rural communities, where people have less exposure to new ideas. All of this was happening long before smartphones and social media. People only knew what they were exposed to. Norah tried to keep this in mind when she was faced with their negative attitudes.

Norah was able to gain a lot of experience flying in and out of the Alaskan bush, which is what the very remote areas of Alaska are called. She had to deal with primitive navigation aids and airports and poor weather. Visibility could be difficult in the conditions she flew in. She also often had to deal with emergencies such as loss of electrical power. On these flights in and out of the Alaskan bush, Norah delivered medicine to villages ravaged by illness, and she delivered Christmas presents to children and dropped necessary supplies for dogsled teams. Once she even helped a miner stuck on a tiny dirt strip in the middle of nowhere. Norah had seen him signaling her as she flew past. She flew him to a doctor and, later, brought him and his supplies back. Another time, she flew a minister around to his congregation for a week. She was not amused when he insisted on blessing the flight. He got out of the plane and prayed over it, making the sign of the cross at the end.

She hoped it wasn't just because he was flying with a woman pilot! Norah told herself that the minister probably blessed whatever vehicle he was traveling in, and she took it all in stride. During one flight, a goose hit the airplane, causing a huge dent and a lot of noise and vibrations. Norah was grateful when she landed safely in Fairbanks.

In the mid-1970s, the building of the Alaskan pipeline was a big deal, and lots of journalists came to Alaska for the story. Originally, only men worked on the pipeline, but eventually, women worked on it, too. As a result, journalists were excited to see and write about the women working on the pipeline. The women did the same jobs that the men did, and they worked long hours, sun up to sun down.

Pilots like Norah had to fly these journalists around, and it became tiring to the flight crews. Well-known journalist Geraldo Rivera arrived to do a story about the women working on the pipeline once when Norah was flying as copilot. Typically, on their trips around the pipeline, the flight crews would cross the Arctic Circle, a circle of latitude on maps. Everything north of the circle is the polar Arctic. They generally would fly fairly low so that the passengers could see the pipeline well. For fun, though, the captain of this particular flight had developed a special "Arctic Circle crossing ride," and he started to climb, to fly the plane higher. The journalists complained that they couldn't see well, but the captain explained that it was necessary to have a little extra altitude for crossing the Arctic Circle and told them to buckle their seat belts because there was often turbulence when crossing the Arctic Circle. The plane rose steeply, pushing everyone against the backs of their seats. Then, the airplane descended very quickly, causing everyone to feel weightless for a moment. Then, it was up again and down again. This happened a few times before the captain announced that they had safely crossed over. The captain held back a sly smile, and Norah looked out her window so that the passengers didn't see her smiling, too. It was the captain's way of creating a little entertainment, to break up the monotony of flying these journalists all around. The journalists did not seem to catch on.

A lot of the guys that Norah flew with in Alaska were applying for pilot jobs with the airlines. The economy was improving after a slump, and the airlines were going to start hiring again. They had been waiting, and so had Norah. The time had finally come. Norah's boyfriend encouraged her to apply to the airlines, too. His job in Alaska would be ending soon, and he would be returning to Washington State; he hoped Norah would come with him. However, because she had grown tired of passengers complaining about having a woman for their pilot, Norah decided to forgo the airlines and only apply to cargo companies.

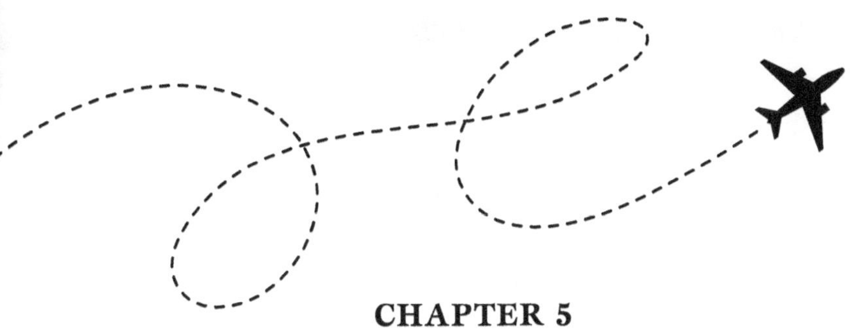

CHAPTER 5

Charlotte Wall

CHARLOTTE WALL WAS born in 1949 in the panhandle of Texas. Her father was a crop duster, and her mother was a homemaker. A crop duster is a person who sprays crops with fungicides or insecticides from an airplane. After three children and years of moving around the country as they followed the crops that needed to be sprayed, Charlotte's mother had had enough and divorced Charlotte's father. Since they were in the Miami area at the time, that is where she stayed to raise her three girls, including Charlotte, by herself.

Charlotte spent many summers with her father and was introduced to the cockpit in a Piper Cub he had borrowed to take her flying in. The plane was at a small grassy field surrounded by trees. That is the precise moment that Charlotte caught the "flying bug"—the desire to fly. From that moment on, she dreamed of being a crop duster like her father.

However, by the time she completed high school, the flying dream was still just a dream. She hadn't yet had any flying lessons and, like many young adults in the late 1960s, she was at a loss as to what do with her life. After an interview with Eastern Airlines for a flight attendant job, which she did not get, Charlotte once again dreamt of being in the cockpit of a plane. She knew with certainty that she wanted to be a pilot.

With renewed ambition and direction, Charlotte completed the two-year career pilot program at Miami Dade Junior College, receiving basic flight training at Burnside-Ott Aviation Training School in Opa-locka, Florida. By 1970, when she was twenty years old, she was a flight instructor at the then brand-new Tamiami Airport in South Miami.

In the mid-1970s, jobs were scarce for pilots. Due to the end of the Vietnam War, with many military pilots now back to civilian life, there were many unemployed pilots. Specifically, there were many *male* unemployed pilots, and male pilots would not take kindly to a woman being hired in "their" place. Furthermore, the requirements for an airline job looked to be beyond Charlotte's reach. However, she would not give up. In order to even be considered by an airline, she needed to be able to fly larger multi-engine airplanes, and she would also have to earn a college degree. She focused first on trying to build up some flight time in multi-engine planes. She didn't have any luck at the Miami airports. The male pilots who were home from Vietnam seemed to have filled all the flying jobs. She needed to expand her horizons.

Fortunately for her, Charlotte was nothing if not resourceful! She hitched a ride on an air freighter heading down to San Juan, Puerto Rico. She had friends who flew commuters around Puerto Rico and the surrounding islands; she thought that maybe they could help her get a job. She ended up not needing their help, though. Her first day there, she landed a job flying a British Norman Islander, a light utility, twin-engine aircraft, for a small company called North Cay Airways. They needed pilots but only recruited locally, so the pilot had to be in Puerto Rico to be offered the job. Odds finally seemed to be in Charlotte's favor.

Flying the Islander was fun for Charlotte. One of the islands she flew to was Isla de Culebra, a small island east of Puerto Rico. The Navy used one end of the island for bombing training, an activity which required pilots to sometimes land downwind. If the bombing range was not active, though, the pilots could make the approach to the runway by flying through the mountain pass and making a hard right turn. The people who traveled in and out of Culebra were mostly locals, as it was not a tourist destination at that time. The passengers would often have their prayer beads out and would be working them when they went through the mountain pass since it could be a little frightening. Charlotte, however, thought it was great fun!

It was not long before she had the opportunity to check out the right seat on the DC-3. The "right seat" meant that she would be flying as first officer, or copilot. How great was that! This was precisely the kind of experience that airline companies wanted. Not only was she getting multi-engine flight time, but Charlotte was also getting "heavy" flying time, meaning that she was flying an aircraft of over 12,500 pounds. She was beyond excited—this was exactly what she needed and the reason she had come to Puerto Rico.

After a year in Puerto Rico, Charlotte's time at North Cay Airways ended. The pilots went on strike for better pay and working conditions, shutting the company down. Charlotte decided to go home and, as she had a year before, hopped a freighter to get back to Miami.

Back in Miami with much more experience than she had before, Charlotte was able to find a job quickly. She would be flying for a small cargo company as first officer (copilot) on a DC-7. This was her first four-engine aircraft, and she was excited to fly it.

For Charlotte, this is when the fun really began! They took off out of Miami, with a crew of five and the boss's girlfriend. On board were two tons of Class A explosives and a spare engine. It was a dangerous load, which thrilled Charlotte all the more. They dropped the load of dynamite in Tehran, Iran, for an oil company, and then made their way to India, where Charlotte would be based for the next year.

With this cargo company, Charlotte and the crew mostly flew live sheep and vegetables from India to Dubai in the United Arab Emirates. However, there was one especially exciting charter in which they flew horses—along with the horses' handlers—from Bombay, which is now called Mumbai, to Oman so that they could be used in a parade. There were no toilet facilities on the plane so they had what's called a honey bucket or can. The honey bucket was always in the back, but for this particular trip, they had relocated it to between the fuselage, or wall of the plane, and the pen for the horses. Charlotte had to slide into the narrow passageway to take care of business, which wasn't a big deal until one horse threatened to kick her. Charlotte was stuck then, unable to get back out for fear of being kicked. Someone finally wondered where the copilot had gone and went to investigate. With help, they were able to settle the horse so that Charlotte could leave the area. This is just one of the many stories Charlotte could tell you about flying cargo in the old days; it was not a job for the meek, that is for sure. Charlotte flew charters all over the world, including to Greece, Pakistan, Afghanistan, Russia, and even to Samarkand, a city in Uzbekistan.

Back in Florida in November of 1974, Charlotte was again looking for a flying job. One of the places she checked was Bush

Aviation. Mary Bush knew of Charlotte because both of their dads were crop dusters. Crews were being put together for a flight of ten DC-3's. Mary and Charlotte applied to fly one of the planes and were accepted. The crews were to fly out to Tucson, Arizona, where the DC-3 planes were in storage at Davis Monthan Air Force Base. Davis Monthan Air Force Base was the biggest aviation storage facility in the United States, and probably the world, and was called a boneyard. It was called a boneyard because the planes that were stored there were so old. The planes that Mary and Charlotte and the other crews were going to fly had been bought by a local government agency and were to be flown back to Lee County, Florida. Charlotte Wall and Mary Bush would fly one of the DC-3's together. This was a big deal—a turning point for both Charlotte and Mary—since both of them were female. Generally, the main pilot, or captain, would be male, and if he was accompanied by a female, she would be the copilot. It was nearly unheard of in the mid-1970s for both the pilot and copilot to be female.

Mary and Charlotte got the green light for takeoff from the David Monthan Air Force Base control tower. Eager to get going, Mary swung the DC-3 out onto the runway and shoved the power levers forward. Charlotte, as copilot, locked the tail wheel and scanned the instrument panel as they rolled down the runway. They both held their breath for a moment because it was the first time that the airplane had been flown in more than a decade. It was like using an old computer for the first time in years—they had no idea if it would work. Everything seemed fine though. The sounds and noises they heard were ordinary sounds and noises. At around 55 knots, which is similar to about 65 mph, the tail of the stripped-down DC-3 popped up. Charlotte called out the takeoff speed and Mary lifted off. They were on their way!

The desert landscape and "boneyard" slipped away. Charlotte and Mary followed railroads and other landmarks, which helped guide them, and they arrived without incident in Lee County, Florida.

Even with all the fun and adventure that she was having, Charlotte still desperately wanted an airline job. Sometimes, though, it seemed impossible, like reaching for something that was never quite within grasp. She had ratings and experience, but it still wasn't enough. A four-year college degree was also a requirement for most airline pilot jobs. Charlotte had been able to save a little money, but she moved back in with her mother to help with finances. Then, with her eye still on becoming an airline pilot, she enrolled in the then brand-new Florida International University.

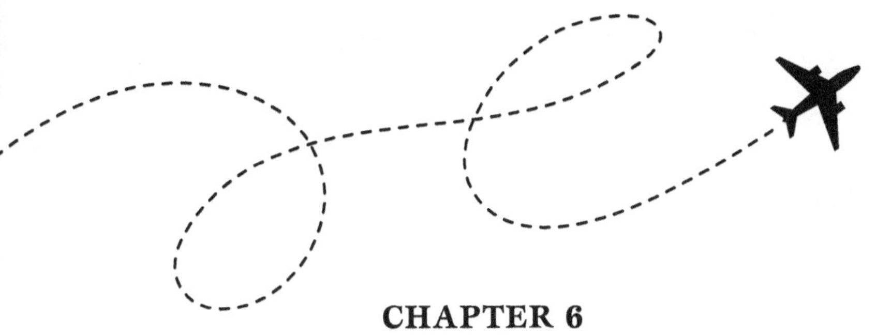

CHAPTER 6

Jill E. Brown

BORN IN BALTIMORE in 1950, Jill Elaine Brown, a classic beauty with a winning smile, grew up in an upper middle-class African American family. Her parents owned a construction company in the Baltimore area, and by the age of eleven, Jill was driving a forklift at her family's company. By seventeen, she was taking flying lessons with other family members. She had caught the "flying bug" and became the first in the family to earn her private license.

At her mother's suggestion, Jill entered the University of Maryland and earned a home economics degree. After graduation, Jill became a schoolteacher. In her spare time, she flew her family's single-engine Piper Cherokee to get flying practice. When she flew around her hometown, the cares of the day just fell away and she was left with the exquisite joy of flight as well as the immediate feeling of competency and fulfillment that comes from a flight well-executed.

In the early 1970s, even though she was happy and successful, Jill thought about flying for a living; she wondered if she could. In 1972, though, there were still no women airline pilots, Black or white. Still, Jill's eyes looked skyward. The planes she was capable of flying included a J-3 Cub, a PA-28, and a single-engine Piper Cherokee. Would she manage to get a job with an airline? Could she be the first Black woman airline pilot?

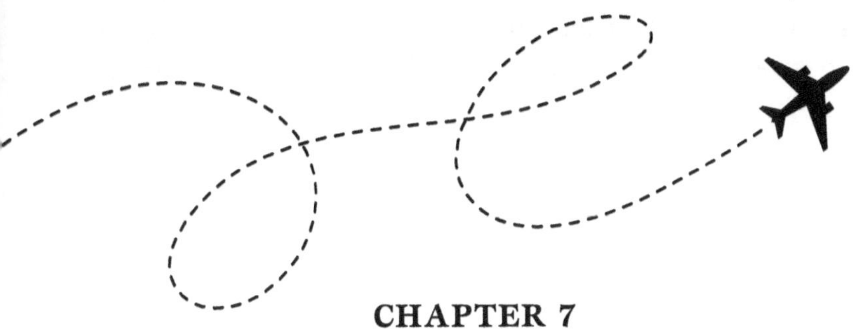

CHAPTER 7

The Laws of Change

THE PATH TO having women in the cockpit of an airplane can be traced back to 1911, when a young female aviator named Ruth Law asked Orville Wright, one of the famous Wright brothers, to teach her to fly, and he said no. He said that women were not mechanically inclined and, therefore, did not have the mental capacity for flying. But Ruth Law learned to fly anyway; she just didn't learn from the Wright brothers.[1]

Another woman aviation pioneer was Harriett Quimby, who in 1911 was the first woman to earn a pilot's license in the United States; she learned to fly at a school in Hampstead, New York, a privilege that many aspiring female pilots would not have had.

Even though the Wright brothers did not want women flying—did not believe they could—many women did, in fact, learn to fly. But they couldn't make a living at it; that was

---

[1] See article by Eliza McGraw, *Smithsonian*, March 22, 2017.

saved for men. Women could be in air shows or air races or do advertising. Even the renowned aviation pioneer Amelia Earhart, who tried very hard to create acceptance for women in aviation, never made a living at flying. It was her books and speaking engagements that earned her money and paid for her flying.

In anticipation of World War II, Franklin Delano Roosevelt, who served as President of the United States from 1933 to 1945, started a Civilian Pilot Training Program. Mary Bush's father trained pilots for the program, which targeted college students. The program started in 1939 and allowed one woman for every ten men selected. However, graduates of the program were required to fly in the military; therefore, once war was declared, the women were excluded from the program since no woman could serve as a pilot in the military. The Civilian Pilot Training Program ended in 1944 after having trained 435,000 pilots, 2,500 of whom were women. Some of those women became Women Airforce Service Pilots, or WASPs. The WASPs consisted of 1,074 civilian (non-military) women who ferried or tested planes for the military from 1942 to 1944. The WASP program ended amid controversy, but one thing was certain: women would not be welcome as military pilots.

At the end of the war, there was a surplus of male pilots. The U.S. Department of Commerce passed a law stating that if women flew passengers, it could only be in good weather because they were required to fly using visual flight rules (VFR). The WASPs had flown using visual flight rules when ferrying planes for the military. The male pilots had no such rule, and flew in all kinds of weather. That rule alone would keep women out of the airline cockpit for another twenty years.

In 1963, the year before the important Civil Rights Act was passed, Betty Friedan published her bestselling book

The Feminine Mystique, which discussed women's feelings of unhappiness and lack of fulfillment. Many women could identify with the book, spurring the formation of the National Organization for Women, or NOW, and starting a movement to improve women's lives.

Then, in 1964, the long awaited, long fought over Civil Rights Act passed. This was a landmark civil rights and labor law prohibiting discrimination on the basis of race, color, religion, sex, or nationality. The following year, the Equal Employment Opportunity Commission (EEOC) was established to administer and enforce Title VII of the new law. In theory, this legislation would finally allow women to be pilots for major airlines, but would that be the reality?

Even after the cockpit was theoretically open for women, the military and the airlines refused to hire women, citing company policy. The airlines were not the only businesses that would not hire women; many others in the fields of engineering, law, medicine, and business held their ground also. It was clear that many places would have to be forced to hire women; they wouldn't willingly do so.

In 1970, led by Betty Friedan, women marched down Fifth Avenue in New York City, demanding that some of those reluctant corporations hire women. Pressure on such corporations increased, and those businesses finally began to make changes. It's hard to imagine now how restricted women's lives were fifty or sixty years ago. For example, women could not have a bank account or a credit card until the 1974 Equal Credit Opportunity Act passed. Before the 1978 Pregnancy Discrimination Act, women could be fired or paid less if they became pregnant. Sexual harassment, a form of abuse or bullying, was not immediately recognized by the Equal Employment Opportunity Commission. That meant that sexual harassment was *not* illegal; men were *allowed* to make women uncomfortable by saying and doing inappropriate things. Men acted with impunity, meaning that they had freedom to say and do what they wanted.

In the 1960s and 1970s, many colleges were for men only. Princeton and Yale did not accept women until 1969; Harvard, 1977. Military academies started accepting women in 1976. Prior to 1973, women were only allowed in the military as nurses or support staff. Jury duty was even restricted by state until 1973, meaning that in some states, women were not allowed to serve on a jury. Birth control was another area where the right to choose was fought over for many years and is, in some ways, still being fought over. The availability of birth control meant that a woman could complete her education, have a career, and plan her own life.

In the book *Because of Sex*, author Gillian Thomas writes: "The legal and cultural change affected by Title VII [of the Civil Rights Act] has been nothing short of revolutionary. The right to remain employed during pregnancy, the right to be a working mother, the right to hold a job historically deemed for 'men only,' the right to be assessed on one's own merit rather than group traits, the right to be free from the indignity of sexual harassment, the right to look and act like *oneself*, whether that's traditionally 'feminine' or something else: all of these advances and more are owed to Title VII.... It's not an overstatement to say that the law is transforming what it means to a woman who works; it is also transforming what it means simply to be a woman."

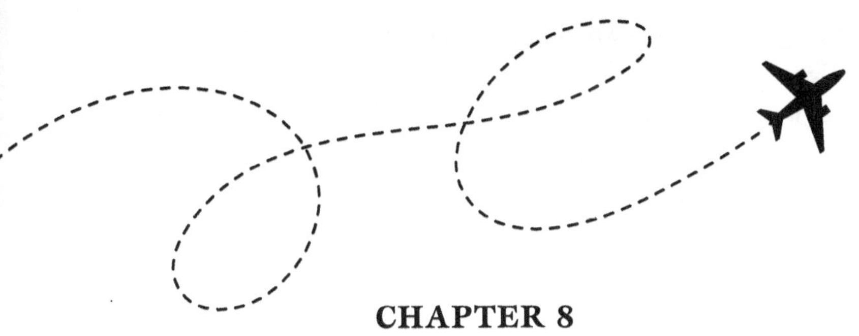

CHAPTER 8

The Airlines Will Never Hire a Woman

EACH YEAR FROM 1968 to 1973, Emily Warner applied to all three of the airlines based in Denver where she lived: United, Continental, and Frontier. As she continued to get more flying time and experience, she updated her application. However, she was continually dismissed and rejected, even though she was well qualified, probably more so than many of the men applying for the same airline jobs—the same men she was teaching to fly.

If she asked about when the airlines might consider hiring a woman, she always got the same answer: "The airlines will never hire a woman." The closest she came to being hired was in September 1972. She heard Frontier was hiring and rushed right over with an updated application. When she handed in her application, the human resources assistant—the person in charge of managing the hiring process—asked her how many flight hours she had. Emily replied that she had 7,000 flight hours, and surprise showed on the face of the human resources assistant; most of the men had fewer hours. Emily's application was immediately taken into the inner office. It was passed around until it made its way to the chief pilot's office, where a final decision would be made. There it sat.

In the January 1973 issue of *Harper's Bazaar*, Emily read about another female pilot who also was hoping to be hired by the airlines; her name was Bonnie Tiburzi. The article about Bonnie motivated Emily, who suddenly realized that she needed to be more assertive if she was ever going to get hired. She had been taught, as many women had, to be demure—to be reserved and modest, what some called "ladylike." To not be pushy. But now she decided she needed to be more forceful. She would stake her claim.

Out of the three airlines based in Denver, Frontier Airlines had always had a special place in Emily's heart. She decided that's where she most wanted to work. She remembered watching DC-3's with Christmas lights lit up flying past her bedroom window at night during the holidays. It had always been a comforting sight when she was growing up. She was determined to set up an interview with Frontier, and this time she would not accept no for an answer. She called a friend at Frontier and told him that she wanted an interview with the chief pilot. Her friend helped her arrange the interview.

Emily went over to Frontier's offices to meet with Ed O'Neil, the chief pilot. Ed was aware of Emily, her persistence and her skill; aviation friends had been encouraging him to hire her for several years. Ed was also aware that new government regulations would make it increasingly difficult for airlines to avoid hiring minorities and women, something they had avoided doing for so long. He too had read the recent magazine article. To Ed, Emily seemed very capable as a pilot. She had 7,000 flight hours and an Airline Transport Rating certificate. He had watched her career progress and knew that she had trained many of his pilots. However, he still needed to officially confirm her ability. He also wanted to make sure that she would be able to get along well with all the men. After interviewing her, he decided that she had the strength of character needed to be a pilot at his airline.

By 1973, Emily was mother to a young child, so another concern Ed had was childcare. Emily explained that her mother and ex-husband lived close by and would be able to provide childcare on short notice. Satisfied with that response, Ed then wanted to ensure that Emily had the physical strength necessary to handle a jet in a variety of conditions and emergencies. They headed over to the simulator, which is a machine designed to provide a realistic imitation of flying an airplane, somewhat similar to a video game. For the next two hours in the simulator, Emily was confronted with every possible emergency that could occur on an airplane. Emily focused on the simulator, intent on doing her best. She believed that Ed and the other pilots would be happy if she failed, as if they were just waiting to say, "See, I told you so."

But Emily worked hard to master the problems in the simulator. She could handle flying on one engine just fine, as would happen if an engine went out, and she easily handled all of the other emergencies Ed dreamed up, too. Finally, as though trying to think of anything else that would discourage her, Ed pointed out that she would be taking a pay cut. Emily said that although that was true, she would be gaining a seniority number, which was worth the loss in pay as far as she was concerned. To her, a seniority number was protection of fair treatment and pay. A seniority number was based on age and date of hire and meant that she would have rank, or priority, over many of the pilots that she was hired with as well as anyone hired after her.

Ed's thought was that if he had to hire a woman pilot—if the airline couldn't avoid it because of the new laws—then that woman might as well be Emily and they might as well be the first airline to do so. With that, Ed O'Neil told Emily the job was hers if she wanted it. She took it.

The hurdles Emily faced, though, didn't stop upon her being hired. Pilots are on probation for their first year. This probationary period allows a company a chance to see if a new employee is going to work out well; if there are signs that the new employee is not a good fit, then the company has the opportunity to let that new employee go. Assuming, though, that the employee *is* a good fit, after the employee's successful probationary period, members of the pilots' union must vote for the pilot to be admitted to the Air Line Pilots Association (ALPA). In Emily's case, some of the members were very vocal, saying that they would not approve admission of a woman into their union. If Emily was not accepted into the union, though, she would not be able to stay as a pilot with Frontier. Something similar had happened on December 13, 1934, when female pilot Helen Richey had gotten hired by Central Airlines. In November 1935, less than a year later, Helen had to leave the job because the union would not allow her to join.

The day of the vote, Emily waited nervously until the decision was made. Fortunately, the "yes" votes outnumbered the "no" votes. Emily was allowed to stay. With that, Emily became one of the first female pilots in the United States to be a member of ALPA.

Whether she was *the* first permanent woman airline pilot for a major airline or not, though, was up for debate. Others weren't far behind.

Bonnie Tiburzi got a call from American Airlines for a job interview in February 1973. Perhaps the airline management had seen the article in *Harper's Bazaar* just as Emily had.

American Airlines flew Bonnie out to their training facility in Dallas, Texas. The airline gave her a short twenty-minute general knowledge test, a physical, and an interview. In the interview, Bonnie talked about her flying experience and showed her knowledge of the history of American Airlines, which she had researched. Bonnie then went back to Florida to her instructing and flying jobs. A few weeks later she received a Western Union telegram letting her know that she had been hired! Bonnie was thrilled.

Bonnie was to report to training on March 30, 1973. At the time she was hired, her flight experience included 1,400 hours of flight time, a commercial flight rating certificate, an instrument rating, a multi-engine rating, glider and tow plane ratings, a single-engine seaplane rating, and a primary, advanced, and multi-engine flight instructor's rating.

Bonnie considered herself to be the first woman airline pilot for a major airline, but Emily believed she was. Who was actually the first? Did it matter that Emily's airline was smaller than Bonnie's? Some seemed to think it did and cited Bonnie as the first. The two women pioneers had many discussions over the years, neither backing down from their position. The Smithsonian Museum put an end to the debate, acknowledging Emily as the first permanent female pilot for a scheduled U.S. passenger airline. It would be nice to think Emily thanked Bonnie for giving her that extra push.

A few other female pilots were also hired by commercial airlines in 1973. One of these was Joy Walker, hired by Delta Airlines. In college, Joy's major had been engineering. One of her professors, a pilot, had encouraged her to learn to fly, and

Joy loved it. She worked several jobs to pay for flying lessons and finally earned her licenses. To build flight time, she taught others and flew in Africa. Flying in Africa helped her to get experience in heavy multi-engine planes, the types of airplanes that airlines wanted to see on applications.

Another pilot, Cheryl Peters, grew up in Roanoke, Virginia, with dreams of becoming a flight attendant, which she did. But one year when her airline was on strike and she wasn't working, she began taking flying lessons in Miami, Florida. When the strike was over, she went back to work as a flight attendant but continued to fly. By 1974, she had earned enough flight time to apply to Piedmont Airlines and became their first female pilot.

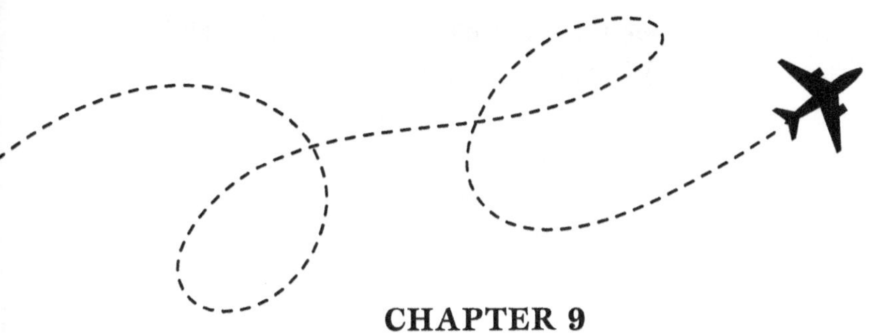

CHAPTER 9

The Quiet Revolution

THE UNITED STATES experienced a recession in 1974 and 1975. That means that there was a downturn in the economy. Employment was way down; not as many companies were hiring. For that reason, very few women moved into jobs that were once held by men because employers favored hiring a man over a woman. Employers believed that men deserved the jobs more than women did. However, the National Organization for Women (NOW) and other similar organizations were working to ensure that when hiring started up again in full force, women would be there on the front lines of change, getting their fair shake.

To help out with this goal, the Equal Employment Opportunity Commission, also known as the EEOC, said that companies wishing to apply for government contracts must have minorities and women making up ten percent or more of their employee base. In other words, there was a lot of pressure on companies to hire at least some women and minorities. In

1976, when corporations started to hire again, the National Organization of Women was watching to make sure women were given the opportunities they deserved. Indeed, women did start to be hired in earnest into otherwise traditionally male-dominated jobs; this period of time is referred to as the beginning of the Quiet Revolution for women. This is the time when commercial airlines in the United States finally started to hire women pilots.

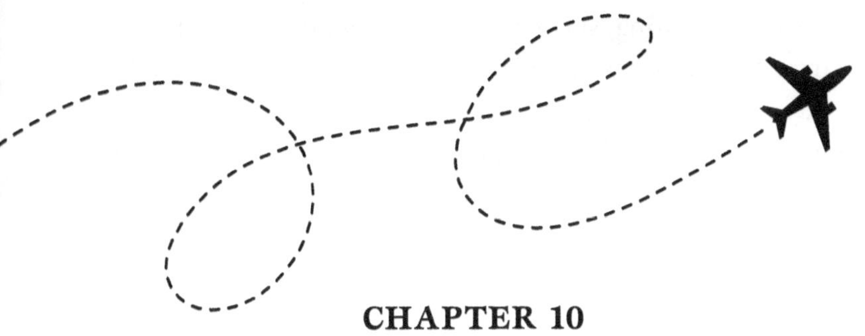

CHAPTER 10

Another Empty Kitchen

IN 1975, MARY Bush had just graduated with a bachelor's degree from Florida International University; she had 3,000 flight hours and had acquired her Airline Transport Pilot certification the year before and was certified to fly DC-3 and C-46 airplanes. She sent out her resume to fifty different airlines, vowing to accept the first job that was offered to her. In January of 1976, Hughes Airwest called her, inviting her out for an interview. Hughes Airwest was owned by Howard Hughes, a well-known businessman, film director, and record-setting pilot. The airline flew up and down the west coast, flying as far north as Calgary, Canada, and as far south as Puerto Vallarta, Mexico.

Mary arrived at the San Francisco airport with high hopes. She was nervous and excited: her very first interview after years of preparation and hard work! To get an interview felt to her like her hard work was finally being recognized and valued. She was picked up from the airport by a hotel van. The following morning, she went to the headquarters of Hughes Airwest. Mary interviewed before a panel of pilots who talked to her about her qualifications and about her experiences flying around the Caribbean. She was surprised to also be asked very personal questions, questions about her private life and whether she was planning to have children. Nowadays, it is illegal to ask such personal questions of prospective employees.

The pilots also wanted to know how Mary might handle resentment from other pilots, and they wondered how she would deal with the harassment and bullying she was sure to face being the only woman pilot. Mary allayed their fears and put them at ease by saying that she was used to difficult pilots; she would handle any situation just as she had in Florida: with grace and patience.

Next, there was a physical test and a personality test. Mary stayed in San Francisco over the weekend. On Monday, she was hired. She couldn't believe it! She had been one of 3,000 applicants for only 40 pilot jobs, and they were offering *her* a job! After so many rejections and people telling her that she didn't stand a chance as a female pilot, she was given a class start date for training for the job. It would be the first class of new airline pilots for Hughes Airwest in seven years. Mary was looking forward to being part of the airline family; it was a dream come true. She was sure that she would be working with high-caliber pilots—respectable people—and she looked forward to it. She was also excited because she would be able to help her family financially. Elated, Mary seemed to float back to Florida, unable to believe her good fortune. There were times that she had to pinch herself to make sure it was really happening.

Around this same time in 1976, Norah was also making some important decisions. After dealing with complaints from the passengers she had been flying around the Alaskan bush, many of whom were horrified to have a woman pilot, Norah had decided that she wanted to fly with a cargo-only company; the ever-present undertone of scorn she had faced had dissuaded her from flying passengers. Some of the pilots she knew were applying to Flying Tigers, a cargo airline, so she decided to apply there as well.

A few weeks after applying, Norah was invited to Los Angeles for an interview. She wanted to be prepared, so she brushed up on interview questions she had heard other pilots talking about. And, indeed, they asked about her flying time, and she produced her log books and pay stubs so that they could verify her flight hours.

But they had a few more questions. Norah imagined that they might ask her technical questions about the plane or about approaches or weather operations. Instead, though, she was asked personal questions about her body.

One of the pilots asked if she would have to take time off from work when it was her "time of the month."

Norah, stunned, looked at them in disbelief. Such personal questions were none of their business. However, in the 1920s, the Department of Commerce had deemed it unsafe for a menstruating woman to fly. Although there was no study done and no supporting evidence or facts, it was still a commonly held belief among male pilots in the 1970s.

The men also wanted to know if Norah would be having kids and, if so, if she would be taking time off to raise her children. They wanted to know if she drank alcohol and what she would do if a pilot made a pass at her. They asked her how she would handle prejudice and discrimination in the cockpit. Discrimination is when people are treated differently because of who they are—for example, if they are a woman or of a different ethnicity.

Although Norah did not like this line of questioning—it made her uncomfortable—she answered all of their questions. Then she went back to Alaska to fly and wait.

Months later, when Norah hadn't heard anything and had therefore decided that they were not going to hire her, she got the phone call that she knew would change her life. Flying Tigers hired her! Thrilled, she reported to Los Angeles for ground school in December of 1976.

Several other female pilots were also hired by airline companies in 1976. One of them was Terry Rinehart. Terry's mother had been a WASP in World War II and had ferried aircraft all over the United States, later receiving the Congressional Medal of Honor for her service. Terry had followed in her footsteps, learning to fly at sixteen, and attributed her aviation successes to her mentors, which included her parents.

Another woman, Valerie Walker Petrie, had announced at eight years old that she wanted to be a pilot. Valerie's dad, a movie star, hoped his daughter would grow out of this wanting-to-fly phase, but as soon as she was old enough, Valerie started working to pay for flying lessons. She became a flight instructor at age nineteen. To build flight hours, she flew in Botswana, South Africa. She also flew a helicopter.

Both Terry Reinhart and Valerie Walker were hired as pilots by Western Airlines and started on the same day in 1976. Among their other similarities was the fact that they were both six feet tall!

By the end of 1976, twenty-two women pilots were scattered around the United States flying for the airlines. While this number was just a drop in the bucket considering that there were many thousands of male airline pilots, the list continued to grow.

Charlotte, like many other women pilots, had been convinced that the airlines would never hire a woman. She had a change of attitude, though, after Emily was hired. Because airlines preferred pilots with college degrees, ideally in engineering, Charlotte went to Florida International University and received a bachelor of science degree in engineering. After earning her degree, she sent out resumes and visited some of the airlines' human resources (HR) departments, the departments that take care of the hiring. Like Mary, she decided she would accept the first job offered to her, since she wasn't sure there would be a second. When she learned that Southern Airways, a local commuter airline, was hiring, Charlotte saw this as a great opportunity since they did not have a woman pilot yet. She hurried right over to their offices in Palm Beach and applied. She was hired as their first woman pilot in 1977.

Mary Hirsch was hired by Continental Airlines in February 1977, when she was 35. She flew as first officer on the DC-9. Before getting hired by Continental, Mary Hirsch had been a flight instructor and commercial pilot who ferried planes around the United States. She was elated to be flying for an airline at last.

Jill Elaine Brown was hired by Texas International Airlines as the first African American woman pilot in 1978 at the age of twenty-eight. In 1974, Jill had applied to and was accepted into the Navy's flight program. It was an honor, yet she found it to be a lonely and unfriendly place for a young African American woman at that time. The men were officers but not gentlemen. Discrimination was rampant, even though it was often covert and not immediately obvious to others. After six months, she left. She still loved to fly, though, so she got a job at Wheeler Airlines, a Black-owned airline in North Carolina. Wheeler provided just the right kind of nurturing environment for Jill, and she thrived. In such a friendly and caring atmosphere, she was able to build her flight time, leading up to her eventual success getting hired at Texas International Airlines in 1978.

In 1978, Gail Gorski was the first woman hired by United Airlines, a full ten years after Emily had first applied there in 1968. Gail Gorski, a former Kentucky Derby Queen, was born in Kentucky in 1952. She had been introduced to flight by a coworker at McDonalds who took her for her first plane ride when she was 16. That was when she knew what she wanted to do with her life. After high school, she earned her private pilot's license, and then she went off to college at Southeastern Oklahoma State University, where she earned an aviation degree. After graduation, she took a job with the Federal Aviation Administration (FAA) since, at that time, airlines were not yet hiring women pilots. She would have to wait a few more years.

Northwest Orient Airlines hired Abigail Davis in 1979 as their first woman pilot. Abigail had graduated from Ithaca College in 1972 with a double degree in English and philosophy and had no plans of learning to fly. The urge to fly hit her after an introductory flight in New Haven, Connecticut, where she was working as a legal assistant. After earning all her ratings, she began building hours as a corporate copilot. In the late 1970s, she interviewed with several airlines before being hired by Northwest. After fourteen years, she retired medically as an Airbus A320 captain. A medical retirement occurs when one has a medical condition that interferes with job performance.

In 1976, Jackie Gero was hired by Ozark Airlines as their first woman pilot. In 1980, she was upgraded to captain on the F-27. "I love it!" Jackie said. "I wouldn't pass it up for anything in the world. It's a hobby you've been able to turn into a job. How many people can say that?"

As more women airline pilots filled the sky throughout the 1970s and beyond, male pilots were often heard saying, "There's another empty kitchen somewhere," referring to the women pilots in their midst. As more and more women began to take to the skies at the airlines, the resistance from men pilots was unmistakable. It was especially noticeable to the female pilots themselves.

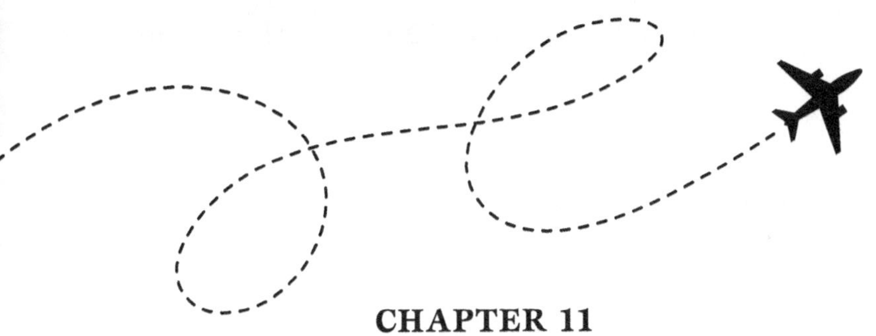

CHAPTER 11

Don't Let Her Pass

EMILY, BORN AND raised in Denver, was able to live at her home during her training at Frontier; this was a special treat since pilots often had to relocate for training. She was given her seniority number, based on her age, the first day of training, and she cherished it. Because it had taken her so long to get hired, she was older than most of her classmates, all males. This meant she was senior to them and would advance to captain before them. As such, she knew that they may even someday fly copilot for her. They knew that, too, and it did not sit well with them.

Emily took the training sessions in stride, training as a second officer on the Boeing 737. The second officer was the person who sat between the captain (pilot) and first officer (copilot) on a small seat that bridged the two pilots. The position of second officer has since been eliminated from flights, but at that time, as second officer, Emily's job was to monitor the instruments and fuel use and to assist the pilots.

Many pilots at the airline hoped Emily would fail training.

- - - - - -

American Airlines had their training center near Dallas, Texas. Bonnie arrived and found out she had a roommate! They were not used to booking rooms for a woman and had accidentally paired her in a room with another pilot trainee, a male. The hotel corrected the problem, amidst a few snickers and stares. Bonnie trained as a flight engineer on the Boeing 727. A flight engineer does not fly the airplane because that's the captain and copilot's job, but the flight engineer has many other important duties to ensure a smooth trip. They are responsible for inspecting the aircraft and making sure it is in airworthy condition and that surfaces are not damaged. There could also be unusual drips of oil or hydraulic fluid or other liquids that need to be investigated. Inside the cockpit, a flight engineer monitors the aircraft systems, fixing technical problems as they arise, and assists the pilots.

During training, Bonnie was given a test. The new test was created after Bonnie was hired. It was for anyone under 5'10" tall and weighing less than 140 pounds. It was designed to ensure that a pilot was strong enough to handle a two-engine-out emergency when flying a four-engine plane, like the DC-8. Certification requires the plane be able to fly and land safely on two engines. For the test, the instructor simulated two engines being out on the same side of the plane; Bonnie had to fly the crippled plane to the airport and land. Bonnie handled this emergency just fine. However, *if* Bonnie had failed to fly well and had failed to successfully land the simulator with two engines out on the same side, she would have been fired before she had even begun. All pilots are hired with a caveat: if you don't perform well your first year, you're fired, no questions asked. And airlines were especially looking for any reason to fire a woman pilot. They were looking for any reason to justify women not being pilots at all.

The captain who was responsible for training Bonnie had her do one extra-day line check trip with him as a test; he wanted to be able to defend his position of her performance in case others complained about her. While Bonnie felt demeaned by this extra training requirement, she also saw it as an opportunity for her to meet more people in the large American Airlines system.

Resistance to her being there was obvious. Bonnie had heard someone say, "Are they really going to let her pass the training?" And when she did pass, they said that she just squeaked by or, worse, "They had to let her through because she's a woman." It wasn't just men who resisted; not all women welcomed the change either. Once a woman wrote to the CEO of American Airlines, complaining that Bonnie had taken a job from her husband. The CEO asked Bonnie to write the woman back.

Pilots sometimes made unkind remarks loud enough for Bonnie to hear. For example, as one pilot passed by Bonnie in the cafeteria, he said, "Eastern is hiring." The implied meaning was that Bonnie should leave American Airlines and apply at Eastern instead. He wanted her out. Some wanted her out, but it seemed that others supported her, too. Either way, nothing would deter Bonnie.

- - - - - - -

Mary arrived in Phoenix, Arizona, on May 9, 1976, excited to be starting her airline career, certain she would be working with the best of the best. The crews in training stayed at a hotel near Arizona State University. When she arrived, Mary saw many of the same men she had seen during her interview. It turned out that many of them were captains' sons, which had probably helped them get hired, but it was still nice to see some familiar faces. Mary greeted them enthusiastically, hoping she would find a friend or two among them.

On Monday, the new pilots rode over to the general offices that housed the training department. Mary would train as a first officer on the Fairchild F-27, a large turbo twin-engine plane which seats about forty people. It replaced the DC-3 and was a mid-range, short-field airplane. It was faster than the DC-3 and had an updated cabin.

During the training, Mary heard many of the same complaints that other women pilots heard.

"Don't let her pass ground school," they said.

And when she passed ground school, they said, "Don't let her pass flight training."

And when she passed flight training, they said, "Don't let her pass the line check."

Some even made threats. "We'll take care of her on the line," they said to the flight instructors.

Later they would ask crew scheduling not to schedule her with them.

Mary let their comments roll off her back. After all, she had heard similar grumbles before. She was determined to show them that she was good, that she deserved this job. Her mentors back in Florida had told her to let her flying speak for itself, so that's what she planned to do.

Most of these new women airline pilots enjoyed their training. For one thing, they were excited to be in their positions.

But also, there was an air of fairness to the training that they appreciated. That is to say: there was an air of fairness to it *until there wasn't anymore*. Some of these pioneering women—those who were among the first to be hired by commercial airlines—told stories of non-standard check rides or other injustices. The men often became smug and arrogant.

For Mary, the intellectual part of training was pure joy. She loved the training itself. Socially, though, she struggled. She tried her best to fit in and be friendly, even when she felt isolated. Even when the men were unfriendly. There was six weeks of ground school, which included written and oral exams, and then there was flight training. For Mary, the Fairchild F-27 was easy to fly. The biggest difference between the transports she had flown in Florida and the F-27 was that it was a prop jet, so cruise speed was faster. Mary did well in all phases of training.

In 1976, flight training was done in an airplane, not a simulator. The planes for training were available between midnight and 8 a.m. Mary and her training partner would show up at 10 p.m. to go over what they would be working on that evening and discuss the expected performance for each maneuver. Each student had two hours of flight time. Another two hours was to be spent observing from outside of the cockpit. You could learn a great deal by watching the other students fly through their sequences. Each training segment had a certain number of procedures that had to be completed, and it was helpful to know what was coming next. Mary had read and reread *Fly the Wing* by Jim Webb, an essential book for pilots, so she was well prepared. She also got along well with her training partner and thought of him as a friend. Later, though, she found out he did not like her or having a female training partner. It was with considerable sadness that Mary experienced either overt unfriendliness or silent hostility, no matter how friendly and prepared she was.

- - - - - -

Norah reported to Los Angeles in November 1976 for her DC-8 flight engineer training at Flying Tigers. It would be her first jet, and she was excited.

Flight engineer training was challenging. Having primarily flown light twin-engine planes in the Alaskan bush, Norah had never encountered a plane like the DC-8. But she had good study habits and was disciplined in preparing for class each day. Even so, the subject matter was sometimes over her head. Flying out of Fairbanks to the Alaskan bush had been a different type of challenge, as it was more seat-of-your pants flying. She had learned to solve any problems that arose, from weather, airports, and loading, to fuel and dealing with passengers; since few services existed in the rural communities of Alaska, all responsibility had been on her. The DC-8, though, with its complex systems, presented a different kind of challenge. However, Norah persevered. She was determined.

Some of the male pilots who had not been hired at Flying Tigers, as well as their wives, were quite outspoken about the fact that a woman was hired in their place. Norah was surprised and hurt by the unwelcome comments. These pilots claimed that they were passed over for someone who was less qualified and who had only been hired because of the quota system, part of the new legal regulations. Their wives even called Norah and chewed her out for taking a job away from a family man. Her room and car were broken into. Items were damaged and stolen. People she had never met hated her. It was very disheartening, but Norah knew that she had earned her position. Sometimes when people are angry about something, their anger becomes displaced and they take it out on the wrong person. That these men didn't get hired was not Norah's fault.

- - - - - -

Elsewhere, Charlotte reported to Southern Airways for initial training on the Metroliner. The class she was hired into consisted of twenty people; all but two were military. She was the only woman and smack dab in the middle of the class as far as age and flying experience. The military pilots stuck together, so she was left out of most conversations and after-training get-togethers.

Despite the fact that Charlotte, Norah, Mary, and countless other women were well-qualified for the job, many people made the assumption that they were not competent or experienced or prepared enough, often claiming that they had stolen a job from a male pilot. It was an outrageous statement, dismissive of the years of hard work and training the women had put into flying. It would be like a competitive gymnast who has put years of work into their sport being told they didn't deserve to compete because only a man could win a gymnastics award. If it sounds ludicrous, it's because it is. Even so, it goes without saying that none of the women would have been hired without the laws that were passed in their favor. Regardless, it was still competitive, and the women still had to earn their positions. Flight qualifications, experience, and a college degree were all required. They were not hired merely because they were women.

In Charlotte's case, the male pilots went to the training department to make it clear that they thought Charlotte would need extra help, even before they ever flew with her. Such "concern" felt like a vague type of discrimination, though Charlotte couldn't quite say why at the time.

It is difficult to put into words the vague harassment Charlotte experienced. Sometimes it would be as innocuous as stopping a conversation when she approached. Other times, it was more obvious, like when the men would empty out her mailbox—a clear kind of bullying. Most especially infuriating was the amount of pornography and lewd pictures Charlotte would encounter in the cockpit, pictures that the pilots would make a point of showing to her. Although she didn't know how to label it at the time, she was experiencing sexual harassment at its worst.

It was a time of social transition for everyone. Many of the men found working side by side with women pilots a challenge, as there were new expectations, both socially and professionally. It was especially hard for men who thought that women should only serve them coffee, not fly a plane.

It was not until years later, after many more women were hired as airline pilots, that the working environment improved. The older men were then no longer threatened by a woman who could fly, and the younger men simply learned to live with women in the cockpit. Times were changing everywhere.

- - - - - -

Jill E. Brown enjoyed training as first officer on the DC-9 at Texas International Airlines and grew to love flying the quick and responsive jet, where the most important skill was organization. She found she always had to think ahead, to be mentally out in front of the airplane. While the flying was good, her working environment, as the other pioneering women had discovered, was not. Overall, she lacked support as both a woman and an African American. During training, the guys would often get together to study and grab something to eat, but no one invited her to join them. On the bright side, though, she had passed training, which was something many of them had hoped she would not do.

Education has an inherent fairness to it; if everyone is in the same training facility, they are, more or less, given the same training and the same opportunities. It was for this reason that the women, having gotten this far, enjoyed their training. After all, they only had to do as well as the men, both in training and in the cockpit, to be viewed as equals—at least theoretically. Everyone took training seriously and came to class prepared. However, in general, the women shouldered another burden—one of having to prove themselves. As such, they would be the first to show up to class and would come to both class and flight training overprepared. Aside from that extra burden, though, training went well, and they were excited to finally fly jets. A jet is an expensive plane that back then, in general aviation, most pilots didn't have access to. Small business jets are more common today.

Even as the women were excited for this next phase of their careers, some airline training departments still tried, and in some cases succeeded, to fire women pilots during training. They would overload them with emergencies in a simulator or training flight, causing them to fail the check ride. But for most of the women, the mantra heard around the airline of "Don't let her pass" was just an empty threat. They often passed their training with flying colors.

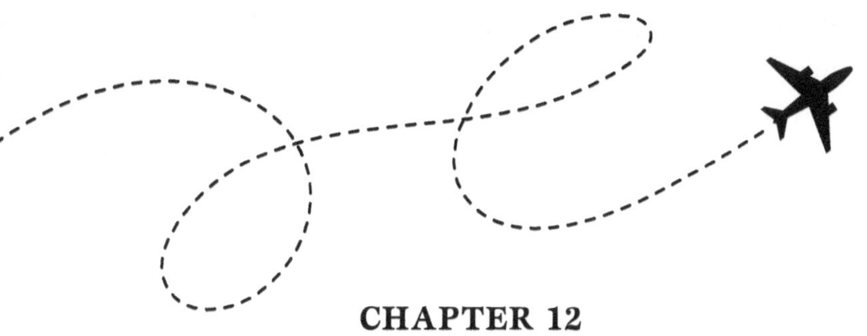

CHAPTER 12

Tales from Flying the Line

FOR MANY OF the male flight crews, a woman in the cockpit took some getting used to. Skepticism and doubt pervaded the ranks: Could women really do the job? In February 1973, on Emily's second trip as a second officer on the B737, the captain told her, "Don't touch a thing on this airplane." So Emily sat on her seat with her hands folded, touching nothing, just as he requested. At the end of the day, she thanked him for a good trip.

Emily soon upgraded from second officer to first officer on the Twin Otter, which meant she was now able to help fly the airplane, assisting with takeoff and landing. It was a much smaller airplane, but it was still an opportunity to pilot a plane. She became captain on the Twin Otter in 1976. It was an easy transition for her because she had had such an extensive background before joining the airline. She also relished being in charge. Years later, when she was back on the Boeing 737 as first officer, the captain asked Emily to go take a seat in the cabin for a while; he wanted to entertain one of the flight attendants. Although Emily was furious, she complied with his request. Captains were not used to being told no back then; Emily felt that she had no choice. She sat in the back and fumed while he entertained the flight attendant up front.

The term "flying the line" is slang for being a pilot on an airline. As pilots who flew the line, the women would be assigned to different captains and crews, depending on the day. Because some captains did not appreciate the fact that they had to fly with female pilots, they would often treat them badly, not letting them do their job, just as those captains did with Emily—telling her do nothing or to relocate out of the cockpit for part of the flight.

Emily flew the line between 1973 and 1990, first at Frontier Airlines, then at Continental, and finally at United Parcel Service (UPS). At Frontier, Emily flew as a captain much of the time and loved it. As captain, she was the main pilot, the one in charge. When asked what she thought her biggest challenge of flying the line was, it was expected she would say something about flying in the winter weather in Colorado. Instead, though, she replied that gender bias was the biggest challenge. Of the thirteen years she flew with Frontier, Emily was captain from 1976 to 1986.

As time went by, all of the airline companies hired more women pilots, and Emily was thrilled that so many women had followed in her footsteps. She was always ready to give a helping hand or a bit of advice to a newly hired woman pilot. However, she had always thought that the new pilots would be her copilots. Unfortunately, this natural order was disrupted because of deregulation (see chapter 14). When the captain on one of her flights was a woman much younger than she, it upset her. She decided it was time to find an airline where she could again fly captain. By 1990, UPS was expanding, so Emily applied to fly captain with them. She would be based in Louisville, Kentucky, and fly captain on a Boeing 727.

Pilots flying the line are exposed to a variety of problems which must be successfully solved. For example, sometimes the equipment does not work right. One night, when Emily was flying as a captain for UPS, they were on their way to JFK airport, the plane fully loaded with cargo, when the rear stairway warning light came on. Emily decided to proceed but flew the plane at a lower altitude in case the rear stairway opened further, which could cause a loss of pressurization and rapid decompression, an emergency situation.

Like anyone, Emily could also make mistakes, but she would always admit it to her crew when she did. For example, one time when arriving in Missoula, Montana, where there are several hills and valleys that tend to look alike, she headed to the airport following the wrong valley. Soon she could not find the airport. Realizing her mistake, she quickly applied full power, raised the gear and went over the hill into the next valley, where she spotted the airport and landed safely.

Other times, the problem can be the weather. Emily, flying as captain on a B727, had to land during a snowstorm in Denver. It was late at night, and the airplane in front of them had previously reported that braking was impossible. According to company rules, Emily could not land under those conditions. But then the pilot of the plane in front of her reported on the radio that "braking is fair to poor," a statement that gave her permission to land. Fortunately, Emily knew the airport well since she had learned to fly there. Another good thing was that the B727 had a good anti-skid braking system. After Emily's plane landed, the airport closed due to the inclement weather.

- - - - - -

Bonnie began her airline career as a second officer, or flight engineer, in 1973 on the Boeing 727; she was based in Boston. She flew the line for about six months before being furloughed in December 1973 due to a slowing economy. Furlough refers to temporary job loss. She stayed on furlough during the recession for the next two and a half years. During that time, she got a good job in Dayton, Ohio. However, her husband was in New York and she didn't like being so far away from him, so she went back to New York where she became a flight instructor at the local airport. Though the pay wasn't very good, she was glad to be back home. When she was called back from furlough, she had returned to her flight engineer position on the B727 out of Boston for a short time before transferring to New York, where she flew that position for the next six years.

Bonnie had the opportunity to fly as copilot on the B727 for about a year, but she was eventually bumped back to her "place in the corner," as she called it, as flight engineer. Then, there were layoffs again. Although she wasn't happy about being in the same position that she had started in eight years earlier, her spirits were lifted when she realized she would not be among the 700 pilots who were once again furloughed. She had seniority now.

In a way, it had been Bonnie's choice to go back to the flight engineer panel. To continue as copilot, she would have had to move and fly out of Dallas, a larger crew base. Bonnie considered herself an Easterner, though, and wanted to stay in New York City. She loved the city and the entire region, and many of her family and friends lived nearby.

In 1983, Bonnie was finally promoted to copilot. In 1987, she upgraded to captain on the B727, and later she was captain on a B757/767.

Some of the daily challenges that Bonnie faced included problems with the pressurization system and with the hydraulic systems of the plane. On one occasion, the motor that put the landing gear down was not working and she had to hand-crank the gear down, much like using a hand-operated well pump like some parks and campgrounds have. It can be tedious and takes a lot of muscle. On another flight, right after takeoff, the left engine got stuck on maximum power and needed to be shut down or turned off. As a result, they returned to the airport on only the other two operating engines. Maximum power is only used for a short time after takeoff, and then a lower power setting must be used. On yet another flight, when she was landing in St. Croix, a bird hit the outside of the right engine, tearing off part of it. Lucky for Bonnie, this was a small tear and did not affect the integrity of the plane's exterior. It was repaired before the next takeoff.

A woman captain was rare and could sometimes be unsettling for male pilots. It seemed to them that it had just been yesterday when women first invaded the cockpit. Now they were in charge and giving orders. And to the chagrin of one junior first officer, Captain Bonnie had to intervene and take over his landing. One of the highlights of the job is the landing. The pilot who has made a successful landing stands at the doorway of the cockpit to say goodbye and accept praise from the deplaning passengers; this is an informal tradition. There would be no such laud and praise for that particular junior first officer.

On another flight, the copilot was luckier. Bonnie had been a flight instructor for years and sometimes it was hard to sit and watch someone else fly in an inefficient or awkward manner. On this particular flight, when a few tips were not enough, Bonnie gave flight instructions to the first officer all the way to the ground. While he was probably not very appreciative of the tips, he got his landing!

Bonnie found that the modern cowboy didn't ride a horse; instead, they flew an airplane. This lone, independent maverick of a man neither wanted nor appreciated the presence of a woman in the cockpit.

Once on a B727 flight into Detroit in which Bonnie was the flight engineer, the tower informed the crew of a wind shift just above the ground. The wind was on their nose as they flew in, and as they got close to the ground, everything looked good. All of the sudden, though, the descent rate increased from 300 to 1,000 feet per minute. That is to say, the wind shift turned out to be more of a wind shear, which was a lot stronger. Power was applied to stabilize the descent rate, and a missed approach was considered. That means that the crew considered flying past the airport without landing and going around again to try for another approach and landing. To have so much extra speed on landing can wear the plane brakes down and is especially hard on the tires. At 100 feet above the ground, the captain took over the airplane and was able to make a safe landing. Bonnie had read about wind shear, a rapid change in direction and speed of the wind, but had never experienced it herself. She was grateful to have had this learning experience as flight engineer before she ever had to confront a wind shear as captain.

Bonnie never knew exactly what to expect from the crews she would fly with, but as time went by, flight attendants and the crews got used to Bonnie. Similarly, Bonnie adjusted to them. In this way, it's not unlike a first day of school, where you meet new people or see people you knew before. Some you're happy to see; some you're not. Female pilots like Bonnie had to adjust to male pilots talking behind their backs but being friendly to their faces. The resentment and negative attitudes tended to stay just below the surface. In this way, while it may be uncomfortable sometimes, at other times things may feel perfectly normal. So when a pilot walked by Bonnie in the crew room and said, "Eastern is hiring," she knew he meant that she should go work there. It hurt Bonnie, but she smiled and said nothing.

After a few years of flying as captain on the Boeing 727, Bonnie moved up to the more advanced members of the fleet, the Boeing 757 and 767. The two airplanes (the 757 and 767) differed in size, but flying the two machines was similar enough that she could get qualified on both at the same time. She would have only one other crew member on the 757/767, instead of the three she had on the 727. As such, the social dynamics would be slightly different.

Her simulator training turned out to be the worst part of her upgrade training. Bonnie had no problem with the actual flying, but she had trouble convincing the simulator instructor that she meant business.

"Bonnie," her instructor would grumble, not hiding his displeasure, "your voice is too soft and what's with this *please* and *thank you* stuff? You get what you want from your crew by demanding it with authority, not by saying please."

He also said things like, "Can't you sit like a man? You know, like you own this machine."

Bonnie had had a similar experience during her initial training as a flight engineer 15 years earlier. She had been the only woman and Captain Boyd Dollar was assigned the task of "getting the girl through the training program." Because Bonnie had been one of the first women pilots hired by the airlines, the press was watching, and the company was watching Captain Boyd. Boyd seemed to consider Bonnie a challenging experiment of sorts. One of the clever examples of his innovative teaching techniques was when he handcrafted two wooden paddles for Bonnie. The wooden blocks measured about 7 inches long and 5 inches wide and a half-inch thick, and there was one red and one white garden glove attached to each block, respectively, the words "right" and "left" on the top. Apparently Boyd had not been happy with the way Bonnie sat in the cockpit seat either, her hands always folded on her lap when she wasn't performing her flight engineer duties. He considered it too "ladylike."

The wooden blocks, though, made folding her hands impossible. Bonnie had loved Boyd's willingness to be a friend as well as a good instructor.

This time, though, the instructor did not seem up for the challenge and didn't want to be her buddy. Instead, he was exasperated by Bonnie's style, or lack thereof.

On one of her very first copilot trips, Bonnie had flown with a captain like this where she had struggled to do everything right. She had been flying the last leg of their three-day journey, and the winds were blowing out of the north at a steady pace. By the time they were descending into LaGuardia, the captain was on the radio with the control tower and Bonnie was silently reviewing crosswind procedures for landing. The wind would be coming at a 90-degree angle from the left. She repeated in her mind what she needed to do to direct the airplane straight down the center line of the runway. The technique called for high precision, and exact execution meant a flawless touchdown. Less than perfect, on the other hand, could result in the plane skipping from wheel to wheel, rocking the wings and creating a sloppy jolting action, safe but humiliating.

Bonnie didn't know what the captain was thinking or what he felt, but at the exact moment before touchdown, he said firmly, "Flare now." With an extra push on the right rudder pedal and a tighter squeeze on the left aileron, Bonnie pulled back on the elevator and flared. The left wheel kissed the tarmac. At just the proper time, the right wheel glided on as well.

After the last passenger deplaned, the captain and Bonnie walked off the plane and up the jetway together, that long narrow tube that seems to go nowhere. As they parted ways, the captain turned to her and said, "You did a good job, Bonnie. I like flying with you." Then, he smiled and walked away.

Another experience, with Captain Robert Buck, had left Bonnie almost giddy. Captain Buck had been retired from TWA as the most senior pilot when she met him. He was one of the most well-respected airline pilots in the industry and had been in every aspect of the aviation world, even writing valuable must-read books on flying. But once retired, even this icon of aviation had to have a civilian check ride every two years in order to keep his pilot license current. Bonnie was elated and totally intimidated when he picked her as his flight instructor for the check ride. Bonnie couldn't hold back giggles at first. She couldn't imagine teaching Captain Buck anything, but he actually proved to be the perfect student. He listened, asked questions, and learned; he was a true professional. Flying is like most things; there is always something to learn, and there's always room for improvement. Even though she was his teacher that day, Bonnie felt like *she* actually learned from *him*.

Bonnie's simulator instructor on the Boeing 757/767 wasn't buying her style though. He kept shaking his head, sighing, and stomping out of the simulator and down the corridor during the breaks. He was not a warm and cozy sort of guy. Even though there had been 15 years of women airline pilots on the property at that point, he was still stereotyping captains as silver-haired six-foot-tall males with voices two octaves lower than hers. But he may have also felt some resentment towards her; he was not an American Airlines pilot, just an employee. In that way, such social interactions were not all that different for pilots as they are with other things. No matter who they are, people can experience bouts of low self-confidence or jealousy. For some male pilots, it was easy to take these fits of possible jealousy out on the women pilots.

Bonnie had a friend named Bob, with whom she had formed a special bond during her weeks of initial training. They were both based in New York and had flown together a number of times. She respected his opinion and knew he would definitely agree with her that this simulator instructor was a jerk.

Instead, though, Bob said, "Listen, Bonnie. Stop whining and play the game."

Bonnie wondered what game Bob was talking about.

"You're working in a guys' world," Bob said, "so you have to start acting like one of the guys. You have to be more assertive." Bonnie was stunned by this advice.

Bonnie realized that she had to learn to work with these men, no matter what their attitude towards her was. Besides, there was something exciting about flying a high-performance jet, and she was excited! She felt hope.

Bonnie loved flying as a captain on the Boeing 757. The cockpit was soundless, allowing the pilots to sense the wind and the wisps of clouds rushing by. From the cockpit, you could see the ground 30,000 feet below, and you could see the weather patterns, the sunsets, and the moon rising off in the distance. But you couldn't hear a thing. Bonnie loved the silence of it.

Once when she was flying, they were streaking between three separate thunderstorm patterns just 30 miles from New York; she was thinking that they would get on the ground before any of the storms broke, but then the radio crackled and the air-traffic controller said, "American 65, stop there! Just stop there."

Bonnie thought he must be kidding and nearly laughed at the strange request. Neither she nor her copilot had ever received a clearance request like that before. She thought it must be a mistake.

But it wasn't. Apparently, LaGuardia Airport had temporarily run out of room. There was simply no place for their plane to go. It was rush hour in the skies over New York and New Jersey.

Behind the cockpit, in the cabin, 200 passengers snoozed and chatted, thankfully oblivious to the trio of violent storms swirling around the plane.

Bonnie's copilot, Jim, meticulously steered the plane around the storms, watching the sky for cloud openings. He delicately circled the B757 around the rumbling patches of flashing gray clouds to the east while the crystal blue sky to the west was aflame with the setting sun's orange glow. On all sides, the sky exploded with magnificent color and electricity. The mass of the airplane and the force of the wind were both awesome. What a view!

As they circled around in a self-created holding pattern, the storms moved slowly towards the Atlantic, and they began to descend. Bonnie, her copilot, and the flight attendants were a team. They worked together for the passengers' safety. The air traffic controller kept all the airplanes moving towards the airport for landing as the storms moved out to sea.

"American 65, follow the DC-10 two miles ahead, descend to intercept the glide slope for Runway 4, and report the outer marker." Bonnie repeated the approach controller's instructions as a matter of procedure, and Jim maneuvered the plane towards the airport and the final approach for landing. They were almost home.

The air was filled with unspent energy that the thunderstorms had left behind. Jim manually steered the plane to the northeast and called for the final flap setting and landing gear. As the pilot not flying, Bonnie responded by placing the flap lever to the 30-degree position and putting the gear handle down, confirming out loud that both flaps and gear were in their proper place for landing. They were cleared to land.

The 757 was an incredible jet, the Ferrari of big jets, sleek and fast. It demanded a pilot's full and constant attention, but in return, it performed to its maximum potential. There was a heart-stopping instant when the left wing was dangerously close to the ground, the right wing looming above them, and then, suddenly, the airplane jerked to the right. At that point, Captain Bonnie said, "We're going around." She knew they had gotten too close to the DC-10. They were less than two miles from it and had gotten caught in its wake. When a smaller, lighter airplane is following a bigger, heavier one, the lighter one must stay way behind so as to not get caught in the larger one's wake. Proper minimum distance is two miles behind the heavier jet, but three to four miles is better, safer.

Jim was working the controls, and the Boeing 757 finally responded to his inputs. As they rose above the wake of the aircraft in front of them, they began flying normally again.

Bonnie took a breath. She made an announcement to reassure the passengers, who were now, more than ever, eager to land.

Slowly and methodically, Jim weaved the plane through the sapphire blue sky, finally descending onto the tarmac. After such excitement, there is the thrill and satisfaction of a job well done. For Bonnie, it was all in a day's work!

- - - - - -

During her first year of being a first officer with Hughes Airwest, flying on the Fairchild F-27, Mary Bush loved her job. She loved the flying. She was living her dream. There were skeptics, she knew—people around her who doubted that she deserved the job, who didn't deem her worthy of it. But she was determined to win those people over with her skill, one by one. She was optimistic and carefree.

Her job was to fly across the desert to Los Angeles, stopping in Yuma, Arizona, and Palm Springs, California, along the way; and they would spend the night in Santa Barbara, California. They always arrived in Santa Barbara in the dark and left in the dark, so Mary never realized the stunning beauty of that area until on vacation thirty years later.

When male pilots said, "There's a woman in the cockpit," it was said as a warning. Mary didn't know what to think when she first heard such a statement. Yes, it was true: She was a woman, and she was in the cockpit. Some of the captains she worked with purposely tried to make the trip difficult for her, loading her up with a large workload just to see if she could take it. Other captains would not let her fly the plane at all, doing all the work themselves. Others let her do her job as intended but would tell her personal stories that made her uncomfortable. It's never okay for people to offer information about their private lives if they are doing so in an inappropriate and unwelcome way. Yet many of these men did anyway, giving graphic details, often hoping that Mary would blush or smile or maybe even share her own personal stories.

When the men told dirty jokes, Mary would laugh so that they didn't think she was a prude. But she was not amused. She found it difficult to maneuver these strange social situations while also performing an intense job. She was young and perhaps a little naïve; she didn't know how best to respond to the men's uncomfortable banter.

Sometimes the talk was more direct. Once when Mary entered the pilots' lounge, a captain frowned at her and, in a gravelly voice, said, "Women should not be in the cockpit. They should be at home cooking in the kitchen." Mary wasn't sure how to react to those kinds of statements either.

At the end of her first year, Mary had finished her probation, the trial period for new employees, and was upgraded to the DC-9, a promotion that irritated many of the male pilots.

The DC-9 was Mary's first jet. Flying a jet is at the top of most pilots' must-do lists, and so it was for Mary. Flying the jet made Mary happy. At the same time, though, she encountered more intense jealousy from male pilots. Their jealousy and anger at a woman flying a jet played out in a variety of ways. The DC-9 was a coveted craft; Mary was in a coveted position. She had moved up with the "big boys." The problem was that many of the "big boys" were nasty and mean. It was like being a freshman girl in high school and suddenly being surrounded by only seniors, all male.

Despite what others thought of her, though, Mary approached each trip with enthusiasm. Still, every trip presented new social challenges. On a four-day trip to the Bay area, a captain instructed her to only work the radios and do the paperwork, nothing more. "Don't touch anything," he told her; it was an interaction similar to what Emily had also experienced.

Mary worked the radios and did the paperwork for the entire four-day trip. At the end of the trip, there was no debriefing meeting or even a "see you later." The captain simply packed up his flight bag and left. Mary felt like a scolded kid who didn't know what she had done wrong. In fact, she knew she hadn't done anything wrong, which only served to confuse her more.

A few weeks later, there was a note in her mailbox instructing her to see the chief pilot.

The captain, who hadn't let her do anything, had written a letter, called a captain's letter, complaining about her, telling the chief pilot that Mary was incompetent. "What happened?" the chief pilot wanted to know.

Mary was surprised, and said as much to the chief pilot. She told him that she never even flew the aircraft, that the captain had told her to just do the radios and paperwork. She had simply complied with his request.

The chief pilot looked stunned. "Really?"

Captains were important to airline companies; they've always been viewed that way. And captain's letters were a tradition, an effective form of communication used for many years. Once women became pilots, though, the effectiveness of these letters decreased, as the letters became yet another way for captains to covertly discriminate against or bully the women pilots.

Mary asked the chief pilot what the captain had written. "Can I see the letter?" she asked.

But the chief pilot simply said, "No. Company policy."

Another tradition of the cockpit was pornography. Pornography can take many forms, but it generally involves visual material that is explicitly sexual in nature. Once women joined the flight crews, the use of such imagery was intended to make women feel unwelcome and uncomfortable. Nowadays, pornography is not allowed in workplaces. Any sort of joking or imagery that is explicit and can make others uncomfortable is strictly prohibited. However, back in the mid-1970s, the rules were different in the more male-dominated society. When women didn't like the pornography or complained about the images, the pilots actually increased its use. The graphic use of pornography is now considered harassment. Back then, though, Mary and other women had to figure out how to handle the crude and demeaning images and jokes. Sadly, it was everywhere.

Mary also faced more physical kinds of assaults, or bullying. Some of the men forced her to do things she didn't want to do. This is harassment and is unacceptable in today's world. Sometimes it is hard to believe that such behavior was often considered "normal" in the 1970s.

Mary moved from Phoenix to Las Vegas in 1978 in order to fly the Boeing 727. It was a new aircraft, and Mary had never flown a new aircraft. She was thrilled. Because she was often flying parties of gamblers into and out of Las Vegas, the passengers were, on occasion, rowdy.

On one flight, the captain wanted to cruise at 42,000 feet, which is the aircraft ceiling, the highest the B727 could fly. It is rare to fly an aircraft at its ceiling; in most cases, the aircraft must be just about empty to do so. Mary knew that what the captain wanted to do was a bad idea. The flight engineer knew this, too, and told the captain several times that they could not go that high. The captain was in charge, though, and dismissed these warnings.

So, they leveled off at 42,000 feet, and the captain called for cruise power. As soon as he did that, he left the cockpit for a break. Mary kept her eyes trained on the airspeed. It kept bleeding off, falling below the recommended speed. The plane was not maintaining speed because it was up too high. Then, the plane started to shudder, which is the first sign of a stall. If a B727 deep stalls, no recovery is possible and everyone on the plane is at risk. Since the captain was not present, Mary had no choice but to take over the controls, even though she was doing so without the captain's specific order. While descending to a safer altitude, she picked up the mic and requested a lower altitude from the flight center.

"I see you are already descending," the operator said. "What altitude would you like?"

"Let's try 34,000," Mary said.

When the captain finally returned, he played it off, almost as a joke, and said, "Oh, good, I see you are descending." It seemed as though he had purposely put the flight at risk just to see if Mary would take control and correct his error.

Another time, on a routine six-month simulator check ride for a Boeing 727, Mary experienced an out-of-the-ordinary emergency. In a simulator, an instructor or supervisor can create any type of emergency they want to create, simply by pulling circuit breakers.

Without any warning, the instructor said, "I want to try a new non-published emergency." The emergency was already occurring when he said this. He had pulled several major system breakers. Because it was a non-published emergency, it was the kind of emergency that no one ever trained for; more to the point, though, the Boeing 727 would never have an emergency where several systems failed at once since the machine has two backup systems: a secondary system and an emergency system.

The Boeing 727 was the first Boeing aircraft to have entirely power-assisted flight controls. However, in this particular case, the instructor removed that assist as well. The simulator was manageable to fly but very heavy. Mary flew the simulator flight and made a normal landing. Against all odds, she did fine; but it was hard to know whether the instructor was just being mean or if they were testing her strength as well. Perhaps both. If they wanted to know if she could fly the airplane when strength was needed, then she had showed them that she could. The simulator was sluggish, heavy, and sloppy, but it was not much different than a C-46 or the DC-7 that she had flown once without flaps.

Failing a check ride can end a career, so Mary also considered that that may have been the instructor's intention: to edge her out of the cockpit. In this way and others, Mary was bullied as a woman pilot. She was also routinely insulted. She learned the hard way that professionalism and being a good pilot could not overcome some people's discrimination and harassment—or their hatred—toward her.

"How can you stand being the most hated person at the airline?" a flight attendant once asked Mary.

Mary was hurt by this negative energy; she had hoped that the airline would have become a kind of family by now. What more could she do?

On the last leg of a three-day trip flying from Tucson to Phoenix, Mary was the copilot. It was the middle of summer and around 115 degrees on the ground. The heat created a bumpy ride, and then an engine fire warning light came on. The captain immediately shut down the engine. Once the emergency checklist was completed, the captain said, "Well, what should we do now?" Mary suggested restarting the engine and continuing the flight to Phoenix. The engine warning light had come on because it was summer and the temperatures were high; it was simply a false alarm. The captain realized then that he had overreacted, and they restarted the engine and flew on to Phoenix.

In 1981, Mary moved to fly the DC-9 in Seattle, hoping the new route and new plane would be a positive change for her. Norah, also based in Seattle, offered Mary a place to stay, and Mary was happy to catch up with a pilot friend. She was feeling worn down by the stress from the interactions with male pilots who did not seem to consider her worthy of the job.

Norah's first assignment with Flying Tigers had been as a flight engineer on the DC-8, flying around the United States and a few international destinations. Although the airline was a cargo airline, they occasionally had passenger flights. On such flights, Norah had been told that the flight attendants would resent her for becoming a pilot instead of a flight attendant. Sometimes, the animosity that a female pilot faced was not just man against woman but woman against woman.

For her part, Norah ignored the crude pictures and jokes that the male pilots left in the cockpit; she held her head high against such harassment, not knowing what else to do. Later, she was told that the male pilots had hoped to torture her enough that she would just quit and that Flying Tigers would not repeat their "stupid woman pilot experiment." After a year of flying as flight engineer on the DC-8, Norah was upgraded to copilot. Training was long and arduous. Then, she had to pass a three-and-a-half-hour simulator check ride in which she was given every emergency possible. Normal check rides last two hours. Her test ended with two engines out on one side and an instrument approach, with two "go-arounds." An instrument approach is when you use instruments in the cockpit to guide you to the airport. The instruments receive signals from the airport. This is different than looking out the window to visually see the airport. Norah successfully landed on the third go-around.

She was complimented by the check pilot, who said, "Don't let anyone ever tell you that you can't fly. Because you can." Still, Norah struggled with believing in herself after all the doubt from others. She wondered how she could get other pilots to recognize her skill and believe in her, too.

On Norah's very first flight on the DC-8 as copilot, the captain looked at her and said, "I do not approve of you being here; it's dangerous." His attitude changed, though, when Norah had to read back extremely complex and difficult flight instructions from their Chicago departure. The captain, having flown with many pilots who had gotten the instructions wrong, was impressed and told her so. He then let her fly the next takeoff and landing. All of these female pilots felt a kind of validation or vindication when their skill was acknowledged. It reminded them of why they chose this path: they loved flying.

Once, when Norah was copilot on a B747, they also had a woman flight engineer. Because he was flying with two women, the captain told everyone that he had a solo flight. These were the kinds of hurtful things that the women pilots had to put up with on a daily basis. In time, these types of remarks added up, often affecting the woman's mental health. No one should have to work in an atmosphere such as that.

Like Mary and like other female pilots, Norah had to prove herself over and over. Many of the pilots acted like she could not fly, and many of the captains had written letters telling the company that she was incompetent.

Once, in a crew room, a captain loudly asked Norah if she wanted a stick of gum, saying, "If you can chew gum and walk in a straight line at the same time, I'll let you fly again." Norah was humiliated. Years later when Norah was the copilot on a flight with the same captain, he apologized, saying that he was just trying to get her to relax a little. His intention had evidently backfired.

Norah wrote a memoir of her experiences as one of the first women pilots, noting, "First women with each airline had taken the heaviest hits. Later women pilots wondered what the firsts were whining about since none of that nasty stuff ever happened to them."

A leading aviation magazine printed its first article about sexual harassment in the cockpit, but the journalist who had interviewed Norah didn't actually use any of her stories for the article, as the stories were considered too extreme to print.

Norah eventually sought counseling because she wanted to learn skills to help her handle the negative vibes from the pilots. Unfortunately, the psychologist said, she couldn't teach Norah "how not to be human."

- - - - - -

Charlotte flew the DC-9 for Southern Airways starting in 1977. She flew out of Miami down to the Caribbean and through the eastern part of the United States. When she upgraded to captain, she was both thrilled and worried. At that time as a female pilot, she felt that no one had her back and if she made a mistake, she would be punished, no matter how small the mistake. Unfortunately, this was not merely paranoia. There were many stories of women failing check rides and being fired. When men failed a check ride, it was often written off as them needing more training, and they were allowed to try again. With the women, though, it was the opposite. It was a very difficult time to be a woman pilot, but thankfully many things have changed since then. Things have changed *because* of these many brave and skillful women. Things have changed because of women pilots who loved to fly.

Jill E. Brown had been ecstatic to be hired by Texas International Airlines in 1978 as the first African American woman pilot. The airline had a fleet of Douglas DC-9's. A DC-9 was a pure jet, bigger and faster than the planes she had flown at Wheeler Airlines. It was her dream to fly jets, but things weren't going as smoothly as she had hoped they would. She saw the way her male classmates were taken under the wing of the older pilots and shown the ropes. But no one stepped forward to mentor her. She became unhappy. Was it the constant publicity photos and interviews for being the first Black woman airline pilot? Maybe she was growing tired of it. Perhaps it was simply the unfriendly atmosphere. It certainly was an altogether different experience than the nurturing atmosphere she had experienced back in North Carolina at Wheeler Airlines.

The following year, 1979, she left and started flying for Zantop International Airlines, a cargo and military charter airline based in Michigan. Started by the Zantop brothers, it served the three main auto companies in Detroit and expanded to have many cargo contracts around the world. Jill found the nonunion atmosphere to be more welcoming than what she had experienced at Texas International Airlines. She worked for Zantop International Airlines until 1985. By then, many women were enjoying airline careers, and as more women became airline pilots, the overall airline environment became more positive for them. For that reason, Jill decided to try again. She knew that other Zantop pilots were being hired by the major airlines. Specifically, United had hired some of the other pilots she knew. So, she applied to United Airlines and waited.

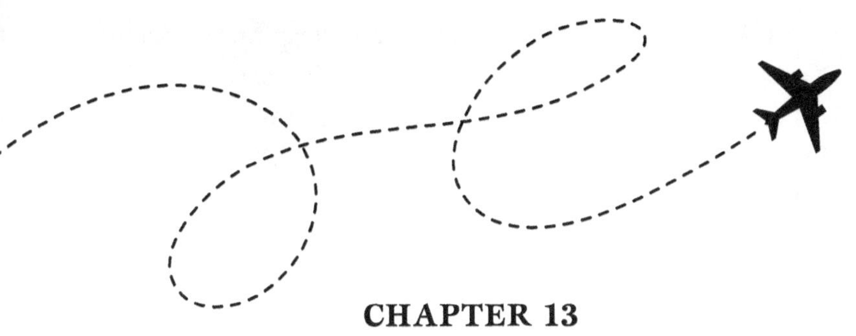

CHAPTER 13

In Emily's Image

A FORTUITOUS MEETING OF Mary Bush Shipko, Beverly Bass, and Stephanie Wallach led to the beginning of the International Society of Women Airline Pilots, ISA+21. They had all been invited by Zonta to D.C.. Zonta International, an organization based in Washington, D.C., is a group of business women that advocates for and empowers women. In January 1978, the group invited women airline pilots to their monthly meeting and dinner since January is Amelia Earhart month at Zonta International. Joining Zonta had been at the top of Amelia's to-do list upon returning from her first flight across the Atlantic. She believed in their mission of empowering women through service and advocacy. To honor Amelia Earhart, Zonta gives out thirty scholarships of $10,000 worldwide each year to women in engineering and aerospace. It was to honor Amelia's work towards equality of women fliers that prompted Zonta to invite newly hired women airline pilots to speak at their January 1978 meeting.

At that time, Mary was flying as first officer on the Boeing 727, a tri-engine jet which carried up to 200 passengers. She was based in Las Vegas and flew the jet to most of the cities Hughes Airwest serviced: Phoenix, Salt Lake City, Seattle, San Francisco, Los Angeles, Puerto Vallarta, and Mazatlan, Mexico.

Charlotte had just been hired by Southern Airways and was based in Miami, Florida, flying as a first officer on the Convair 580, a low-wing medium-stage turbojet that carried around 40 passengers. Charlotte flew around the southern United States. As soon as Mary got the Zonta invitation, she called Charlotte to see if they could meet up together in Washington.

The two of them stayed at the Washington Hilton. Several other women airline pilots also attended the Zonta International meeting.

It was winter and very cold, with lots of black ice on the sidewalks. Mary, who had grown up in Florida and now lived in Las Vegas, was unfamiliar with such ice. Soon after leaving the hotel, she slipped on the ice, falling to her knees. The problem, though, was not getting up, but staying up. She crawled along until she could hold onto a wall, eventually making it back to the hotel. That icy adventure would prove to be a metaphor of sorts for women pilots at the time—trying to keep it together, to stay up, and not continue to fall on the ice. To that end, the women pilots decided they needed to organize in such a way that they could better support each other.

Mary and Charlotte had enjoyed meeting everyone at the Zonta gathering and hoped they could get together every year. The other women pilots thought the same. After all they had been through, the women airline pilots wanted to form an organization of their own through which to support each other. Although they had seen news clippings of each other, had seen each other in the airports, and had heard each other on the flight radios, most of them did not really know each other. They thought it would be nice to develop more solid friendships. After all, they were all women who each could truly understand what it was like to be breaking a gender barrier in a job that had been traditionally for males only.

Since Mary was based in Las Vegas, she suggested that it might be a great place to hold a conference. The other women thought so too. So they planned to have their first conference at the Circus Circus Hotel in May 1978. Letters inviting women pilots to the event were mailed out to all the domestic airlines by a few of the other women. Twenty-one women pilots showed up for that first meeting in May 1978, representing approximately twenty-five percent of all women pilots flying for airlines in the United States at the time. It was an exciting moment for everyone. They looked forward to getting to know each other.

Their meeting started with dinner and drinks at Circus Circus. Then, many of the women went sightseeing or visited the casino tables. The business meeting occurred the next day, when the twenty-one women discussed names for their organization as well as other details.

Several possible names for their new organization were discussed. Some of the women were also members of the Ninety-Nines, an international organization of women pilots; that group's name originated from the number of women pilots who had attended their first meeting.

The women also discussed using acronyms or abbreviations associated with flying. For example, ISA is an acronym that means international standard atmosphere. The international standard atmosphere is the temperature at a given altitude. The women liked the idea of using that acronym because it could also stand for International Society of Women Airline Pilots. With that in mind and to acknowledge the twenty-one women in attendance, they decided on ISA+21 as the name of their organization. ISA+21 would be open to all women airline pilots from around the world. A board was also selected that day, with a chairman rather than a president. The women were uneasy selecting a president, someone they viewed would have power over the other women. For that reason, they preferred more of a round table of board members where all of them would be equal.

The United States in 1978 was conservative; gender roles were still traditionally defined, which is part of the reason that so many of the men pilots had problems with women being in the cockpit. However, where the Ninety-Nines came together to seek equality and be taken seriously, this new organization, ISA+21, sought only friendship and support. The women feared that there could be a backlash if the organization had an agenda beyond friendship and support.

The women did not want their new organization to be viewed as militant or for the women to be negatively stereotyped. The media had made "feminism" a dirty word by 1978, and no one wanted to be viewed in that light. For all these reasons, it was decided that friendship and support would be the main objective of ISA+21. Even today, with the group still going strong, most women join the organization for the friendship and camaraderie. It remains committed to being inclusive.

For some in the group, friendship got off to a slow start. Many of the women had survived the brutal cockpit environment by building walls around themselves emotionally, and they weren't going to immediately let down their guard.

In the group, the women shared their hopes and dreams for the future, talking about the families, husbands, and children most of them were yet to have. They also shared the challenges of the unequal treatment they faced.

Today the ISA+21 mission has been expanded to inspire, support, and advocate for women pilots; in that vein, they offer mentoring and scholarships to rising women pilots. Through the scholarship program, the organization has given over $1,400,000 to young women intent on becoming airline pilots. When Emily Warner passed away in 2020, her image became an icon for the organization; new pins and other products bear her image. Today the organization has 650 members. ISA+21 has requested that Women Airline Pilot's Day be September 21.

In 2015, African American women pilots formed Sisters of the Skies, an organization dedicated to supporting and reaching out to up-and-coming Black women pilots. Similar to ISA+21, they too have programs of mentoring and scholarship, specifically for young African American women.

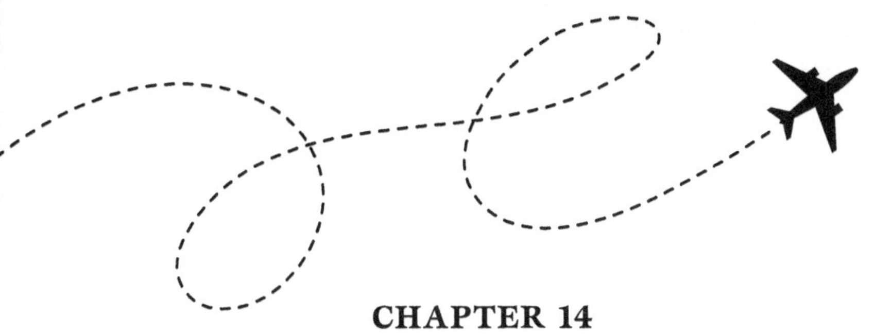

CHAPTER 14

Chicken Feed Fares

DEREGULATION UPENDED AIRLINE travel. The airlines had always been heavily regulated and were considered important to the nation's economy. To that end, a committee called the Civil Aeronautics Board set the fares, routes, and schedules for all airlines. Some people benefited from this regulation, but others, especially passengers who had to pay high ticket prices, wanted a new system. Senator Ted Kennedy felt it was a consumer issue. After much debate, the Airline Deregulation Act of 1978 was signed by President Carter. It removed the rigid regulations of airline travel. Now airlines could fly when they wanted, where they wanted, and they could charge what they wanted.

This deregulation, though, negatively affected many airline workers. Some airlines, such as Eastern and Braniff, went out of business. Many of their employees found work with the new airlines, like Southwest. The airlines started to fly all over the country, offering low fares. Additionally, some people thought that pilots were paid too much. As a result, a new two-tier system, in which junior pilots were paid less, was forced upon the pilots. Another thing that happened was that airlines acquired other airlines, a kind of merging together into one company. When this happened, the acquiring airline generally made the rules, and this was especially reflected in the newly merged seniority lists, which stated which pilots and employees had seniority over others. When someone has seniority, they tend to have more options and more security in their position.

Change came to Emily's life when Continental bought out Frontier in 1986. Her beloved seniority number was pushed closer to the bottom. Continental gave their own pilots, the ones who had been originally hired by Continental, the best slots. Emily, who had flown as a captain with Frontier, was forced back to the position of copilot. She would not have a full thirty-year career in which she retired from Frontier, as she had once dreamed of. This was distressing to her. While deregulation did open the cockpit up wider, giving opportunity to new pilots, it displaced others. United Parcel Service (UPS) was hiring captains, which was very unusual. In most airlines, you were hired on at the bottom and had to work your way up to become captain. Emily couldn't resist. She applied at UPS and was hired as a captain on a B727.

Norah's airline, Flying Tigers, was acquired by Federal Express. Like Emily, Norah was placed at a much lower level of seniority after this acquisition. She was hired as a flight engineer and was eventually moved up to first officer but was never able to fly as a captain. To make matters worse, Federal Express was nonunion, which meant that the working conditions and many of the benefits were not as employee-friendly. For example, Federal Express did not have a pregnancy leave benefit. They disallowed Norah two years of her service time because she had been on pregnancy leave. Federal Express also had different requirements for being available to fly. Cargo airlines fly cargo to a city, and then they may have to wait until new cargo needs to be delivered to a new city. It is the pilot's responsibility to be ready to fly when the company gives them a callout and tells them that it's time. Norah felt that the crew call-out system had draconian consequences at Federal Express. For example, you could be fired if you missed a callout. While it is understandable since the company must depend on its pilots, it was different at Flying Tigers where the union would have protected a worker from being fired for that reason.

At American Airlines, Bonnie was able to move up from flight engineer to copilot after six years, only to be moved back down again the following year, 1982. Plans for her airline to expand were reduced due to competition from new low-fare airlines.

Mary and Charlotte's airlines were merged together, becoming first Republic Airlines and, later, Northwest Airlines. When Howard Hughes died in 1976, Hughes Airwest's parent corporation did not want to own an airline, so it was put up for sale.

Many airlines merged; others went out of business. Pilot pay and retirement benefits were reduced. The hub system sprang to life. Before deregulation, airlines flew nonstop between many cities. After deregulation, though, to increase efficiency, airlines adopted a hub system, in which flights fly into a central airport, known as a hub. At a hub, many people headed for the same destination board the same flight, thereby maximizing aircraft use and increasing passenger loads.

As Senator Ted Kennedy had predicted, deregulation of the airlines led to the democratization of airline flying, meaning that it was more accessible to people. In 1978, Continental Airlines led the way with what was known as their "chicken feed fares," low fares for reduced services. Texas International followed with their "peanut fares." Today there are a variety of low-cost, no-frills airlines that offer cheap seats. Clearly, there were both good and bad things that came out of deregulation.

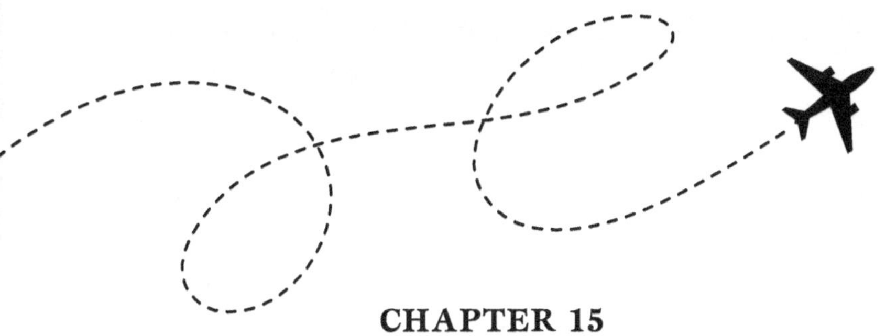

CHAPTER 15

The Civil Rights Act of 1991

A RADIO ANNOUNCER ONCE said, "If someone's hitting you and they have no worry of you hitting them back, they'll just continue to hit you." This was what it was like for many of the early women pilots. There was no oversight, which meant that when the men pilots acted maliciously and cruelly to the women pilots, nobody cared. The men had no fear of punishment, which means they could act with what's called "impunity," saying anything they wanted to say and doing most anything they wanted to do. They had no fear of punishment or consequences. Additionally, for companies, there was no monetary consequence for doing the right thing. Without a financial incentive, change was slow. That meant that these first women pilots had to endure what might be called a free-for-all atmosphere, where anything goes.

All of the early women airline pilots—Emily, Bonnie, Mary, Norah, Charlotte, Jill, and others—experienced sexual harassment and discrimination to varying degrees. Sometimes this awful form of bullying was overt, or obvious; other times, it was covert, or hidden. Women were excluded from what some called a "good old boy" system, a system of intolerance that is often demeaning to women, as "good old boys" tend to think they are superior to women and are fond of the conventional ways, such as women staying home to raise kids. There were exceptions, of course, especially if one of the women flew with a pilot who had flown as a copilot with her father. That pilot then may have had more respect for the woman pilot due to that connection. The majority of airline pilots in the 1970s were still ex-military. If a woman pilot's dad had died in the line of duty, these ex-military men might, and did in a few instances, take the woman under their wing as a kind of mentor. Those women pilots were treated with respect and are a good example of what a nurturing environment can do; for everyone else, though, laws were needed to ensure respect and care.

Effects of the bullying and sexual harassment that many women pilots faced include lowered self-esteem and self-confidence, anxiety, depression, weight loss, and other psychological effects, such as post-traumatic stress disorder, better known as PTSD.

As an added stressor, the women pilots fought not to be characterized as career women or feminists. While these are much more positive terms today, back then they were not. Most of the women, in fact, would say that they were not feminists and probably wouldn't have been hired had they said they were. The women worked hard not to make waves. That is to say, they tried to be agreeable. They didn't want to give any of the men a reason for not liking them. But it hardly mattered. Many of the early women pilots were harassed and discriminated against from the first day they arrived, and there were no laws to prevent it. Sexual harassment as a term was not yet even recognized by the courts. The women tried to be good-natured and take it on the chin, but they hadn't anticipated that their bodies wouldn't cooperate. That is to say, many of them just stuffed their emotions away. Not dealing with your emotions, though, is mentally and physically damaging. For some of these women, stuffing their emotions down would eventually cause a breakdown. These early women often paid a high price for the sexual harassment they had to endure.

The two events that sped change along were the Navy's Tailhook scandal and Anita Hill's testimony before Congress, both of which occurred in 1991. The Navy's Tailhook Convention became a scandal when eighty-three women accused Navy officers of sexual assault. This raised the public's awareness of the environment that women in male-dominated jobs faced. The same was true of Anita Hill's testimony about the harassment she said she experienced while she worked as an aide to Clarence Thomas, a Supreme Court nominee. These two events were catalysts for the Civil Rights Act of 1991, highlighting the need and importance of protecting women against both sexual harassment and gender-based discrimination in the workplace.

Once the Civil Rights Act of 1991 became law, airlines and corporations throughout the United States designed training programs to make sure people were held accountable for their behavior.

A few women pilots brought lawsuits against their airlines for pictures of nude women that male pilots had put in the cockpit, in addition to other unequal treatment they had had to endure. Some of the women won large monetary awards. When Mary was invited to an airline reunion in 2009, a retired pilot told her that a lot had changed after she left. Some of the pilots he knew had to go to court, pay fines, and attend classes on how to behave better. After 1991, the way women were treated was important for companies, and it was too expensive to ignore. Women airline pilots hired after 1991 entered a much more humane cockpit.

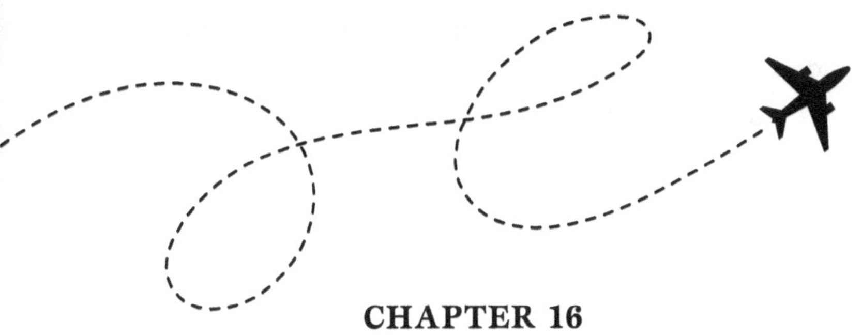

CHAPTER 16

Making Air Travel Safer

ANOTHER CHANGE THAT significantly transformed the working environment of the cockpit in the 1990s was something called Cockpit Resource Management (CRM), also called Crew Resource Management.

In the 1970s, there had been several airliner accidents. How did that happen? How could these new, big, beautiful, and ultra-safe airplanes with triple systems crash? Many airliners had emergency systems in place, so aircraft builders did not want to take the blame for any accidents. Airline companies didn't want to take the blame either; they hired only the best and the brightest pilots, those with arguably the best training in the world. But as skilled as these pilots were, investigators found that it was often pilot error and not mechanical problems that caused these planes to go down.

Naturally, the Federal Aviation Agency (FAA) wanted to increase safety and decrease accidents. In 1979, they had a conference to address the problem. Topics discussed at the conference included how to strengthen cockpit communication and prevent accidents. What was recommended was a set of training procedures that focused on interpersonal communication, leadership, and decision-making skills in the cockpit. The program was meant to encourage teamwork and resource management.

United Airlines had had a crash in 1978 that was due in part to the crew being distracted. While they were troubleshooting a landing gear problem, the plane ran out of gas. This was similar to an Eastern Airlines accident in 1972, which occurred as the crew was trying to get a green indicator light on the nose wheel to come on, a light that would let them know it was locked in place. The failure of the nose wheel to indicate it was locked in place had distracted all three crew members, and they flew the plane into the Everglades. Both accidents should have been avoided. If accidents could be reduced and pilot efficiency improved, all airlines were anxious to adopt the program.

The term "cockpit resource management" was coined by John Lauber, a psychologist. He had the idea of shifting the power structure from a captain-centered model, where what the captain said was accepted without question, to a more team-oriented approach. Many of the captains, many of whom were ex-military pilots, did not like this idea of being told what to do or asking someone with lesser experience for advice. Many first officers were aware of this attitude and tended to say nothing when they disagreed with the captain's actions, unless it could result in an accident. But these old ways had led to a workplace atmosphere that was not conducive to teamwork and, as a result, led to accidents. When women were added to the cockpit, this merely served to exacerbate, or make worse, the lack of teamwork, as many captains viewed the women as inferior pilots.

United Airlines led the way with cockpit resource management. They developed a training program for their crews that focused on communication processes, decision-making, team building, workload management, and situational awareness. Pilots harboring gender bias would have difficulties with one of the basic tenets, mutual respect. As one of the pilots, Captain Gene Swarner, said after Mary was hired by Hughes Airwest:

> "In 1976, I had heard that our company, Hughes Airwest, had hired a female pilot. As a pilot with the company for about 20 years, I was not impressed, as I think I had a bit of a sexist attitude about a woman in the copilot's seat. I didn't much care for the idea of women police or firefighters either. Probably for strength, ability, or lack of either. This also turned out to be just another sexist idea. Well, it was not very long until I came to work one morning and here was a female copilot in my cockpit…. It wasn't long, though, before I realized that Mary was not only very good to work with but she had some natural ability to do the job; some pilots have this ability early in their careers. We soon became good friends, and I didn't have the strength to tell her about my initial attitude toward female pilots. When I retired in 1990, we had 77 female pilots, many of them captains and all doing quite well."

In addition to requiring mutual respect and teamwork, cockpit resource management required overall equality and holding pilots accountable for their actions. While safety may have been the primary reason for the changes, treating colleagues with mutual respect and relying on their input also put an end to male captains telling female pilots not to touch anything or telling them that it was dangerous for them to be there.

Emily spent the last ten years of her career as a Federal Aviation Administration (FAA) inspector who would assess the United Airlines' crews' check rides and rate their cockpit resource management performance. Her experience with the way men abused women in the cockpit made Emily a perfect fit for this position.

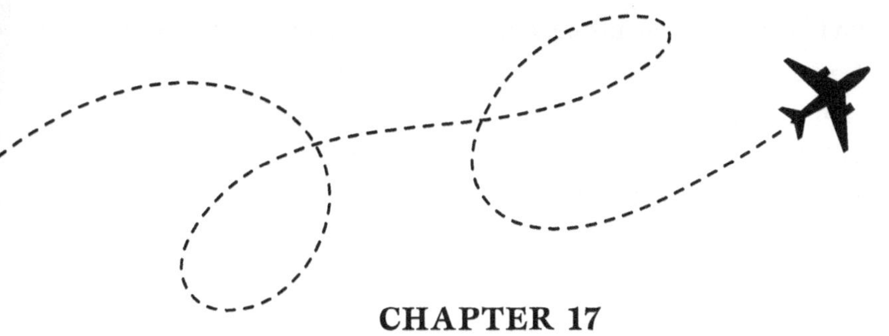

CHAPTER 17

Their Fates

ONCE FRONTIER WAS sold in 1986, Emily flew with Continental for two years. Then she left Continental to fly with United Parcel Service (UPS). She loved flying captain again. However, Emily lived in Denver, Colorado, and was now based in Louisville, Kentucky, which meant that she had to commute to work. This kind of commute was difficult because she needed to start to work a day early, and it could often take another day to return home. So, instead of working for five days, it was more like seven. Therefore, after two years of commuting, she left UPS. In 1990, she went to work for the Federal Aviation Administration (FAA). The FAA is the largest transportation agency of the U.S. government and regulates all aspects of flying. Emily's flying background met the extensive requirements of the position, and her poise and grace won everyone over. As the Aircrew Program Manager for the United Airlines' Boeing 737 fleet, Emily oversaw check rides and safety programs and rated how well crews worked together. She also made sure they were implementing cockpit resource management (CRM) correctly. As a former crew member herself, she was uniquely qualified to assess the nuances and effectiveness of the crews working together. She greeted crews with "I'm from the FAA, and I'm here to help you," and she meant it.

Working at the FAA was a big departure from the days when Emily was flying as a junior second officer and being told not to touch any of the controls. Emily had come full circle and now gave report cards to flight crews. Emily rated the crews on factors that were related to accident prevention and safety. Indirectly, her work diminished gender bias in the cockpit, a topic very important to Emily and all women pilots. How sweet it must have felt to the woman who was once told, "You fly pretty well for a girl."

Emily retired from the FAA in 2002.

Family life for Emily was both rewarding and devastating. With her husband, she had a son, but this first marriage did not work out. She eventually married a man who proved to be a stable and nurturing force in her life. They both loved the Rocky Mountains and flying, and they both had children from a previous marriage.

In retirement, Emily spent her time encouraging and inspiring young women to enter the aviation industry. She told young women that "individually, we are grains of sand; together we become a beach." She believed that with determination and perseverance, a person could achieve almost anything.

Emily passed away in 2020 in Denver, Colorado, and today her pilot's uniform hangs in the Smithsonian National Air and Space Museum. She is recognized all over the world as the first woman airline pilot in the United States.

- - - - - -

Bonnie's life moved forward at a slower pace. She did not want to commute, so she chose to wait until she could land the position she wanted right there in New York. Economic recessions, deregulation, and the airline expanding their other bases while keeping New York the same size all caused Bonnie to wait longer than she would have liked. After being an airline pilot for over ten years, Bonnie reflected on what she really wanted. From an early age, she had had one single focus: to become an airline pilot. Yet for most of the first ten years of her career, she either sat behind the pilots as a flight engineer or was on furlough. Where was the exciting airline job she had dreamed of? When would she finally get to fly the airplane? She knew she could bid for captain or copilot at another base, but she was determined to stay in New York. Bonnie later came to recognize this time of reflection as essential, as it helped her remain true to herself and her dreams. She eventually moved up and was able to spend the last ten years of her career as a captain on a Boeing 757/767.

In the late 1970s, Bonnie had married a pilot, but their marriage was a difficult one and they eventually divorced. Her second marriage, though, was a happy nurturing one. She retired in 1999, leaving flying to raise her children. Today Bonnie is known as the first woman pilot for a major airline. She donated her uniform to the Smithsonian.

- - - - - -

Mary, who at age twenty was going to become an airline pilot or die trying, retired after five and a half years due to medical reasons. She was a DC-9 first officer at the time. Her dream had been crushed, but she had been told by a doctor that she must take time off in order to remain healthy. She had persevered in what is now called a hostile work environment (HWE), and such environments can affect a person both mentally and physically. For what she had endured at the airline, Mary eventually brought a workers' compensation claim against the airline.

Prior to retiring, Mary had gone to the Equal Employment Opportunity Commission (EEOC), where she was told that sexual harassment did not exist. A labor lawyer told her the same thing. The term "sexual harassment" did not become a recognized legal term until 1986.

It took many years for Mary to feel human again, but Mary learned that adversity can teach us. Today she would say that she was not lost when she left, but instead, through a process, leaving helped her to be found.

Mary eventually built a good life with her family, feeling that her quality of life was her personal responsibility. She fought to be happy. Mary went forward, learning to forgive and to embrace the life she has.

- - - - - - -

Norah's boyfriend in Alaska had urged her to get a job flying with an airline. She chose to fly cargo only, and they got married and built a house together in the Seattle area. Norah was gone two weeks every month, flying around the world. Her husband, though, didn't like her flying schedule, and they divorced. Norah's second husband also did not like her being gone so much; the schedule was also hard on their two young children.

Like Mary, Norah retired for medical reasons. It was 1998, and she had put in twenty-two years of service and was flying as first officer on a very large aircraft called a McDonald Douglas MD-11. She was diagnosed with post-traumatic stress disorder (PTSD) and depression. It has taken a long time for society to understand the effects of sexual harassment on people and, specifically, the mental toll it took on many of these pioneering women.

Norah died from cancer in 2017.

- - - - - -

Charlotte also retired for medical reasons. She had been with the airline for 15 years, flying as a captain for the last eight. Like the other women, she also felt unsupported and was worn out; she was also diagnosed with PTSD and depression. Retiring early was difficult for Charlotte, but she has stated that it heals her to read about all the women who came next, pursuing careers in aviation; she loves that women continue to "carry the torch."

Charlotte married another airline pilot, and they were happy for several years. But between flight schedules and commuting schedules, they gradually drifted apart and eventually divorced. Like many PTSD survivors, Charlotte has had difficulty talking or writing about her time in aviation.

- - - - - -

Jill Brown, a bright and gifted pilot, went into the Navy in 1974 and then flew with Texas International Airlines in 1978, long before policies and laws were enacted to rein in some of the more egregious behavior by the male pilots. She had to endure behavior that later African American women pilots did not.

For the first women pilots, their biggest fault was their gender, something they could not control. They paved the way, though, for the next generation of pilots. Today, women pilots can focus on their love of flying without having to deal with the biases and difficulties that the first female pilots had to endure. See Appendix A for an open letter about "firsts."

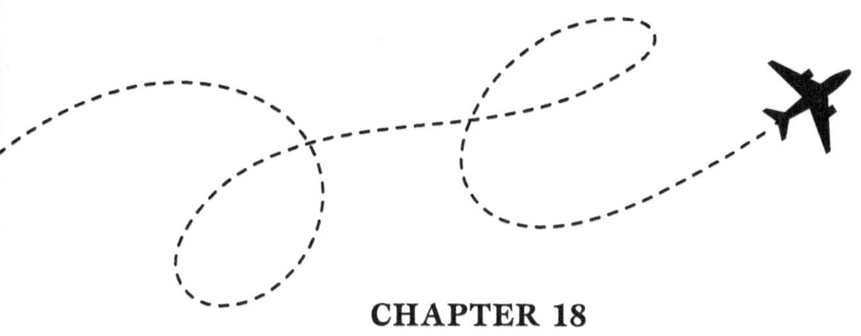

CHAPTER 18

Additional African American Women Airline Pilots

I F WOMEN, IN general, faced resistance as pilots, then African American women faced even greater resistance. It took several years after the first woman was hired by an airline for an African American woman to be hired.

Shirley Tyus Suber, a flight attendant with United since 1972, became United's first African American woman pilot in 1987, nearly ten years after the airline had hired their first female pilot. Shirley started taking flight lessons in 1977, and once she earned her commercial rating, was able to fly for Wheeler Airlines. In order to build the necessary flight time and ratings, Shirley juggled her flight attendant schedule with United, her pilot schedule with Wheeler Airlines, and classes at Embry-Riddle Aeronautical University.

Jill Elaine Brown, initially hired by Texas International Airlines, later applied to United Airlines, where she knew some of the pilots and hoped for a better work environment. When she was not hired by United, she applied again. After three tries, she decided to sue them, as it appeared that they were refusing to hire her simply because she was an African American woman. In 1990, Jill filed a discrimination lawsuit, but she lost the lawsuit, even after an appeal. However, it's possible that she helped pave the way for Melissa, their first hire outside of the company.

Melissa Ward was hired by United Airlines in 1992 as a second officer on the DC-10. Her path to getting hired was one that would not have been possible earlier. After high school, she was awarded an Air Force ROTC scholarship and attended the University of Southern California. She graduated in 1986. After her six-year military service was complete, she was hired by United in 1992. Later she became the first African American woman at United to fly as captain.

Northwest Orient Airlines hired Stephanie Johnson in 1997 as their first African American woman pilot. Stephanie had learned to fly while attending Kent State University in Ohio. In 1997, there were only twelve other African American women airline pilots in the United States. Like other pioneering women, Stephanie found that she did not receive the encouragement from other pilots that males would have been given, and some people seemed to have diminished expectations of her. If she had a bad day, she might be told, "Well, maybe this isn't for you." She stayed the course, though, and in 2016, became Delta Airlines' first African American woman captain.

Delta Airlines had hired Dawn Cook as their first African American woman pilot in 2007. In 2008, Delta merged with Northwest, and Stephanie then had seniority over Dawn. Dawn had attended Embry-Riddle Aeronautical University (Daytona

Beach campus), where she took flight lessons and graduated with all of her flight ratings while completing her college degree at the same time. Her mother, who had been a flight attendant for twenty-five years, inspired her. In 2017, Dawn became manager of a new department at Northwest, in which her job was to reach out to communities and colleges to scout for and encourage future airline employees. In 2017, Stephanie and Dawn flew a flight together, Stephanie as captain and Dawn as first officer.

American Airlines hired Brenda Robinson in 1992 as their first African American woman pilot. In 1977, she had also been the U.S. Navy's first African American woman to attend flight school in Pensacola, Florida. At the airlines, she flew the Boeing 727, 757, and 767. After 17 years as a pilot, she left to run a nonprofit called Aviation Camps of the Carolinas.

Patrice Clarke Washington was hired by UPS in 1988 as a second officer. She was promoted to captain in 1994. Born in 1961 in Nassau, Bahamas, Patrice's love of flying began on summer vacation flights to Miami. In 1979, she enrolled at Embry-Riddle Aeronautical University as the only Black student. In April 1982, she graduated as the first Black woman in the school's history with a bachelor's degree in aeronautical science and her commercial pilot's certification. After graduation, she flew for a small island-hopper airline, eventually going to Bahamasair, an airline headquartered in Nassau.

There were certainly other African American women pilots who helped break the race and gender barriers, but they are not included here due to a lack of information about them. Like others, they may have felt unwelcome by the industry and retired early. To date, African American women pilots only represent around one percent of pilots flying for the airlines.

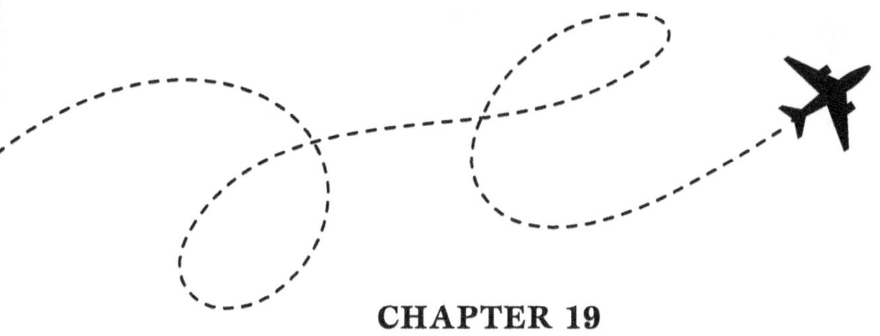

CHAPTER 19

Women Airline Pilots Around the World

Turi Wideroe (Norway)

Turi Wideroe was born in 1937 in Oslo, Norway, the land of the Vikings, where her father would take her flying as a young girl. Norway is known for its beautiful fjords, which are long narrow cuts of water surrounded by steep sides or cliffs. In 1962, while working as a magazine editor, Turi started taking flying lessons. She was looking for adventure.

Following in her father's footsteps, Turi flew seaplanes to the fjords of Norway, carrying both freight and passengers. In 1968, Scandinavian Airlines hired her as a pilot, the first woman pilot in the western world.

Turi went on to receive the Harmon International Trophy for outstanding achievement in Arts and Science and the Amelia Earhart Medal.

Deborah Lawrie (Australia)

Deborah Lawrie was born in 1953 in Sydney, Australia. When she was 14, her dad decided he wanted to learn to fly, and she accompanied him to the airport and helped him learn the checklists and other procedures for flying. She decided she wanted to learn too, and her dad promised to give her two flying lessons as a birthday gift when she was old enough. At sixteen, after her first solo flight, she caught the "flying bug." Her instructor said she took to flying like a fish to water. In 1976, she was trying to get hired by an airline. She filed a lawsuit after repeatedly being denied hiring. She won her suit and was put on the payroll but was not allowed to fly. The airline cited her menstrual cycle as one reason. They also said that her PA announcements would make passengers worry, having a woman piloting the plane. Although she did eventually start flying the line, the airline still contended that an all-male crew was better. In June 2020, she was inducted into the Australian Aviation Hall of Fame.

Melody Millicent Danquah (Ghana)

Melody Millicent Danquah, born in 1937, is considered the first female pilot in Africa, although she did not fly for an airline. Melody was born in Ghana and educated at the Methodist Primary and Middle Schools in Larteh (a town in Ghana) and Wesley Girls High School in Cape Coast. Melody also attended the Government Secretarial School. She learned to fly with the Ghana Air Force. Her solo flight in 1964 was the first by a woman in the Air Force. She served in the Ghana Air Force until retirement in 1984. She received a Long Service Award and an Efficiency Medal.

Saudamini Deshmukh (India)

Saudamini Deshmukh wanted to be a pilot after her first plane ride when she was eight years old, but her family couldn't afford the lessons. Saudamini's goal was to fly over the Taj Mahal. To help reach her goal, she joined the Ninety-Nines in India. As noted earlier, the Ninety-Nines is an organization specifically designed for supporting women pilots around the world.

Through the Ninety-Nines, American women pilots with big hearts and small planes opened up their hearts and homes to help Saudamini, and Saudamini went to the United States to earn her pilot licenses. Afterward, she returned home to India and was hired as India's first woman pilot.

Saudamini's story offers an important reminder to not be afraid to reach out for help when needed. Doing so can help you hold on to your dreams and reach them.

Huda Al Musallami (United Arab Emirates)

Emirates airline's first woman pilot was Huda Al Musallami. Emirates is the largest airline of the United Arab Emirates and is based in Dubai. Huda grew up loving planes and worked first as a flight attendant. She was hired as a pilot in 2004 after graduating from flight academy.

People were very surprised to see an Arab woman as a pilot. Some Arab women weren't allowed to even drive a car, so people wondered how they could fly a plane. Because of such cultural restrictions, Huda had to leave her house before the sun came up so that her neighbors would not see her.

Huda wears a hijab, or head covering, as part of her flight uniform, which she had to fight for to be allowed to wear. It was worth it, though, because it was important to her that she stay true to herself. She believes that everyone should have the freedom to be true to themselves.

Ayesha Rabia (Pakistan)

Ayesha Rabia had big dreams while growing up in Pakistan. She was born in 1947 and flew with her father, who was a doctor. His hobby was flying on the weekends. Ayesha joined a flying club and got a private license at the age of seventeen.

In 1980, Ayesha was hired by Pakistan International Airlines, but then the airline changed its mind. General Zia, the head of the airline, did not like the idea of a woman flying next to a man in the cockpit. So, Ayesha would have to wait nine long years. In the meantime, she worked in the airline's training department. When General Zia died in 1989, Pakistan International Airlines hired Ayesha as a pilot.

In 2005, after flying for many years as copilot, Ayesha became the first female Pakistani captain of a commercial scheduled flight. A year later, she flew the first Pakistani flight with an all-female crew.

Debbie Aw (Republic of Singapore)

Silk Air in Singapore recruited Debbie Aw in 2003 after having turned her down many times before. Debbie's love of flying had begun in 1992 when she joined a flying club at college.

Debbie became a captain in 2012. She began her career with some trepidation, concerned that if she failed, she would make the path even more difficult for other women. However, she now sees attitudes changing and others becoming more accepting of women pilots.

Debbie encourages kids and young adults to learn about the different careers that are available and to not let their gender hold them back. Specifically, she hopes that when more women learn about what being a pilot is like they will want to fly too.

Chinyere Kalu (Federal Republic of Nigeria)

Nigeria has scheduled airline service by other countries, as they do not have an airline of their own. However, they do have a national flight school. Chinyere Kalu, the first female commercial pilot of Nigeria, was raised by a single mother. Chinyere joined the Nigerian College of Aviation Technology in Zaria, Nigeria, in 1978.

Although she learned the basics of how to fly in Nigeria, Chinyere had to travel to the United States and Britain for advanced training. She returned to Nigeria afterward and, in 1980, took an entry-level position at the Nigerian College of Aviation Technology. In 2014, she retired as the president of the college.

In 2007, Chinyere received an International African Achievers Merit Award. She enjoys serving as a mentor and teacher to young women.

Irene Koki Mutungi (Republic of Kenya)

Irene Koki Mutungi, born in Kenya in 1976, was hired by Kenya Airways in 1995. She became a captain in 2004. Her father was a pilot with Kenya Airways, so Irene had decided at the age of five that she wanted to follow in his footsteps. Although he wasn't convinced it was a good idea, he supported her efforts. She went to the United States to earn her commercial flying license and was hired by the airline upon her return to Kenya.

Like all of those who pave the way for others, she had to prove herself, and she worked very hard in order to win acceptance from those around her.

Ari Fuji (Japan)

Ari Fuji developed her love of flight from growing up near a United States air base in Japan. At 155 centimeters tall (just over 5 feet), she was considered too short to attend the Civil Aviation College, so, instead, she earned a degree in law, took a job, and started saving her money. She then went to the United States to learn to fly. In 1999, at the age of thirty-one, she was hired by Japan Airlines. Japan Airlines changed their height requirement when she became captain in 2010, acknowledging that height didn't affect a person's ability to be a good pilot. Knowing that she is setting an example for others, Ari finds extra courage by looking in the mirror and saying to herself, "I am the captain."

Elena Novichkova (Russia)

Elena Novichkova was the first woman captain for Russia's Aeroflot airline. Russia is the largest country in the world, spanning eleven time zones and bordering sixteen countries. To be the first woman captain in such a large country is indeed an accomplishment. She became captain in 2013 for the Airbus

A320. In 2016, she was awarded the Medal of Nesterov, an honor named after a Russian World War I fighter pilot named Pyotr Nikolayevich Nesterov.

Elena is one of only sixty-two female pilots out of 42,000 pilots at Aeroflot.

Han Siyuan (China)

China's Spring Airlines, based in Shanghai, hired Han Siyuan in 2008, and by 2017, she had been made a captain. When she first decided to apply for a job as a pilot cadet in 2008, she was up against 400 female classmates. They took tests that measured everything from their command of English to the length of their legs.

"I've gotten used to living in a man's world," Han has said. In Spring Airlines' promotional videos, Han said that she hoped the growing publicity would help to raise awareness. "I can't personally give people opportunities," she said, "but I hope that [the publicity] can slowly help open the door for companies or for girls with dreams to fly."

Pearl Wendy Mak (Malaysia)

Malaysia Airlines hired Pearl Wendy Mak in 2018. Pearl was picked to be one of the first three women pilots in the airline's new female pilot program. Before that, Pearl had spent the previous 25 years flying for other airlines around the world. At age fifty, though, she was happy to return home to fly over her beautiful Malaysia. She knows that being a woman in a mostly-male industry can come with its challenges. By always doing her part, though, she hopes to create unity as part of a team.

Kalina Milani (Brazil)

Kalina Milani was hired at the Brazilian airline VARIG as their first woman pilot in 1991. She had previously worked for the airline on the ground and as a flight attendant. When Kalina was in high school, her dad had bought a small plane for his business, sparking her interest in learning to fly. But he told her that women did not fly. However, she drew inspiration from visiting the United States in the early 1980s, where she encountered women airline pilots. When she was a little older, she started to work and was able to pay for her own flying lessons. Kalina had hoped to one day fly as a captain at VARIG, but financial troubles at the airline ended that dream. However, she then moved to fly for Emirates, becoming the first woman captain at that airline. She contends that her "office"—the cockpit—is the most beautiful office in the world.

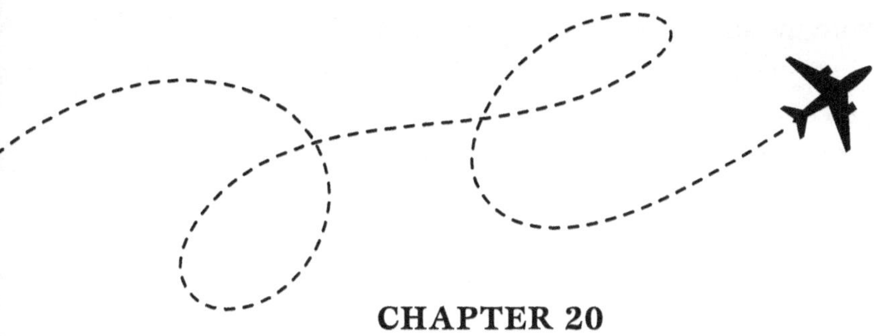

CHAPTER 20

Conclusion and the Future

AT ONE TIME, becoming a woman airline pilot was unattainable—an unreachable goal. This book illuminates the women who were on the front lines of change. We see their dreams, sacrifices, triumphs, and disappointments. Today the cockpit is called a flight deck, and crew members work as a team. Women pilots can indulge in their love of flying without having to worry about navigating a difficult work environment.

Now, in the third decade of the twenty-first century, nearly fifty years after the first woman was hired for the airlines, the industry welcomes females. There are currently 10,000 female pilots worldwide and 5,000 in the United States. Not only are women now welcome, but there have been many other improvements in the industry as well.

Major benefits include overall safer aircraft, improved cockpit communications, and promises of more diversity from most companies. When the pioneering women first started flying with the airlines, over 85 percent of the pilots were military pilots; today, though, military pilots represent fewer than 30 percent of airline pilots. An optimistic vision of the future for women airline pilots is now a reality. Some airlines even sponsor a girls' aviation day as a way to encourage women to pursue a career in aviation.

Three specific developments over the years have made planes safer and friendlier. These are a fly-by-wire (FBW) system, Crew Resource Management (CRM), and Environment, Social, and Corporate Governance (ESG).

Fly-by-wire refers to a purely electrically signaled control system and was first used in 1987 by Airbus. Airbus's A320 took to the skies in 1988 with Air France using the FBW system. Adoption of FBW was slow at first because many pilots and aerospace engineers felt that the best and safest controls are mechanical rather than electrical. However, FBW has become quite popular today. Major benefits of FBW include an envelope of safety, meaning that when the computers deem something dangerous, it is automatically corrected, thereby increasing safety. For example, since 30 percent of air accidents are because of aircraft stalls, programmers restricted the ability of the aircraft to be stalled. Another benefit is reduced pilot workload. Thirty years after its initial introduction, FBW is being instituted into a variety of other aircraft, including private pilot planes.

Crew Resource Management revolutionized the working environment in the cockpit, which is now called the flight deck at most companies. The goal of CRM is to make the flight deck an enjoyable place to work, a place where everybody can contribute ideas and have the opportunity to make a difference—where resources are readily available. The individual components of CRM include communications, situational awareness, problem solving, decision-making, and teamwork. With CRM, all crew members work as a team, sharing mutual concern and responsibility for the flight.

Another development is ESG, meaning that companies are assessed with Environmental, Social, and Corporate Governance (ESG). For example, ESG evaluates companies on their hiring practices, including their level of equality in regards to hiring women and minorities. Companies with better ESG scores are considered better to work for, so this is an added incentive for companies.

The women pilots discussed in this book did not have formal mentors, but now there are mentors who will root you on so that you can reach your dream. Many of the over 10,000 women airline pilots, plus others in the aviation industry, are ready to help. We all need that person (or people) who can help us reach our goals.

In 2020, before COVID-19 disrupted the world, the International Air Transport Association (IATA) made a promise that by 2025, twenty-five percent of their upper management, which includes pilots, will be women. Could you be one of those women?

Over the last 45 years, women airline pilots have done a good job of paving the way for future generations. The women in this book often sacrificed family, relationships, and personal time. They had to overcome many obstacles and persevere to reach their goal. As such, they would like to be an inspiration to young women, encouraging them to fly or pursue other jobs in the aviation industry.

This book has focused on the women pilots who broke the gender barrier in the airline industry, and on behalf of pioneering women everywhere and throughout history, they want to extend a welcoming hand to anyone who might follow them into the sky. As Emily Warner once said, "Individually we are grains of sand; together we become a beach."

Flying is a vocation that comes out of purpose and passion. After only a few flying lessons, you may decide to continue in this occupation, inspiring future generations, as the women in this book have done. Or maybe you will find another way to be a pioneer—to do something that no one else has done. Dare to dream. Dare to inspire.

APPENDIX A

An Open Letter to the Women of Firsts
By Jessica Ruttenber (from her blog *Hidden Barriers*):

In every career field there is a generation of of [sic] Firsts followed by a generation of Next. The security of opportunity afforded to the next generation is possible by the hardships endured by the women of Firsts. Although I am a women [sic] of Next, a second generation wave, I was raised by the generation of Firsts. I can look to my left and see beyond the perseverance of accomplished women that marked their place in history, to the pain of a generation of women who suffered in silence. Survival was priority, complaining was never an option.

Then I look to my right and see the women of Next and even the beginning of a third generation that is hopeful and not defined by gender. They at times take for granted the opportunities open to them. Unlike the Firsts with their "keep my head down" and excel mentality, the "Nexters" believe without question there is no reason they can not achieve their desired success. Because of the path cleared before them, they make no apologies[,] speaking up to remove any barriers in their way. But the truth is that not all barriers are so obvious, they are hidden and often undetected by the women of Next. Their insidious nature can make progress even more difficult[,] often manifested as a subtle impostor syndrome rather than a direct assault.

To the women of first thank you will never be enough. We see you. Some of you have ascended into positions of power, as few of you as there are. You hide your scars well and often play down your pain. Your generation taught you that standing out on the smallest of matters as a women had the potential to take away from your power and bring question to your competence and accomplishments. Each of you have adapted in your own way. Some assimilated into the collective that resented your mere presence or perhaps some of you now carry the sword and shield as a pathfinder for others. Many of you didn't ask to be the first, you simply wanted to pursue your passion and along with it came the burden of discrimination and bias.

APPENDIX B

Courage
by Amelia Earhart
(written while working at the Denison
House as a social worker in 1927)

Courage is the price that Life exacts
for granting peace.
The soul that knows it not
Knows no release from little things:
Knows not the livid loneliness of fear,
Nor mountain heights where bitter
joy can hear
The sound of wings.
How can life grant us boon of living,
compensate
For dull gray ugliness and pregnant
hate
Unless we dare
The soul's dominion? Each time we
make a choice, we pay
With courage to behold the resistless
day,
And count it fair.

APPENDIX C

This poem has been included because many of the
women felt that they took the road less traveled.

The Road Not Taken
by Robert Frost

Two roads diverged in a yellow wood,
And sorry I could not travel both
And be one traveler, long I stood
And looked down one as far as I could
To where it bent in the undergrowth;

Then took the other, as just as fair,
And having perhaps the better claim,
Because it was grassy and wanted wear;
Though as for that the passing there
Had worn them really about the same,

And both that morning equally lay
In leaves no step had trodden black.
Oh, I kept the first for another day!
Yet knowing how way leads on to way,
I doubted if I should ever come back.

I shall be telling this with a sigh
Somewhere ages and ages hence:
Two roads diverged in a wood, and I—
I took the one less traveled by,
And that has made all the difference.

APPENDEX D

Dreams
by Langston Hughes

Hold fast to dreams
For if dreams die
Life is a broken-winged bird
That cannot fly.
Hold fast to dreams
For when dreams go
Life is a barren field
Frozen with snow.

LEGEND OF PLANES FLOWN

Planes in each category are representative of that type of airplane. Not all airplanes discussed in the book are pictured here.

TRAINERS

A plane designed to facilitate flight training of pilots.

The Cessna Skyhawk 172, produced in 1955, is the most popular single-engine airplane for flight training and economical weekend trips. The high wing design gives student pilots better visibility in the air.

The Piper PA-28 Cherokee, produced in 1960, is a family of two-seat or four-seat light aircraft built by Piper Aircraft and designed for flight training, air taxiing, and personal use. The low wing makes crosswind landings easier.

The Cherokee was so popular that Piper created several variations. The Cherokee Six was faster and had a longer range and was often used as an air taxi.

In 1999, CIRRUS produced an airplane with a parachute attached.

It was inspired by developers after they watched NASA bring space capsules to earth with parachutes. It is a popular choice among students.

LIGHT TWIN ENGINE

Small multiengine airplane with a maximum takeoff weight of 6,000 pounds.

The Seneca was developed in 1971 as a twin-engine version of the Piper Cherokee Six. The prototype was a Cherokee Six that had wing-mounted engines installed. A few other modifications were also made. It had better performance and the added safety of two engines. It can carry six passengers.

The Baron was first produced in 1961 by Beechcraft. Olive Ann Beech and her husband founded the company together in 1932. When he passed away, she became CEO. She was the only woman CEO of an aviation company at that time. The Baron is a low-wing, high-performance light twin that can carry six passengers and plenty of luggage.

TRANSPORT AIRPLANES

Large civil airplanes and helicopters.

The Douglas DC-3, built in 1934, is a heavy twin-engine plane that can carry 30 passengers. It was developed for American Airlines. They wanted a plane that had more passenger comfort and safety. It was very helpful during WWII.

FOUR-ENGINE TRANSPORTS

The Douglas DC-6, built in 1946, is a four-engine piston airplane that can carry 100 passengers. It could fly above the weather, giving passengers more comfort and safety. It was developed for use in World War II to move troops and supplies. However, it arrived a bit too late and was refitted for passengers. After jets came, the DC-6 was primarily used for cargo.

The Lockheed Constellation was built in 1943 for TWA airlines. A four-engine piston aircraft, it could carry 95 passengers. It had a range of 3,500 miles.

TURBO-PROP JETS

An airplane with both a propeller and jet engine. Very useful when flying to smaller cities with smaller runways. They can land in a shorter distance, and carry around 30-40 passengers.

DASH 8 The De Havilland Canada DHC-8,[3] commonly known as the Dash 8, is a series of turboprop-powered regional airliners, introduced by de Havilland Canada (DHC) in 1984. it was developed from the Dash 7 with improved cruise performance and lower operational costs. The Dash eight can carry 37 to 90 passengers, depending on the model as some were stretched.

The introduction of the regional jet, (see next plane) altered the sales picture for the Dash 8 and other turboprops. Regional jets allow airlines to operate passenger services more efficiently and cheaply. Turboprop aircraft have lower fuel consumption and can operate from shorter runways than regional jets, but have higher engine maintenance costs, shorter ranges, and slower cruising speeds

REGIONAL OR COMMUTER JETS

Small airliner designed with a short range and carry up to 100 passengers

Bombardier CRJ200 is a regional jet, it started flying 10 May 1991.

It has efficient turbofan engines for lower fuel consumption, increased cruise altitude and speed over its sister the CRJ 100. It can accommodate 52 passengers.

NARROW BODY AIRLINER AND MEDIUM-RANGE JETS

Narrow body airliners have one aisle and a medium travel range.

The Douglas DC-9 is single-aisle medium-range plane. It first flew in 1963. It carries 60 to 120 passengers, depending on aircraft model.

The Boeing 737 is a narrow-body airliner whose first flight was in April 1967. The lengthened 737-200 entered service in April 1968. This airliner evolved through four generations, offering several variants for 85 to 215 passengers. Early models have a range of 3,215 miles.

Boeing 737-900. The Boeing 737 MAX is fourth generation. It has 200 seats, an an extended range of 4,045 miles.

Boeing 757-200 is a twin-engine medium-range jet. It can carry up to 228 passengers and has a range of 4,500 miles and is up to 80 percent more fuel efficient than the older 727 jetliners. The pioneering two-crew computerized flight decks, or "glass cockpits," of the 757 and 767 are nearly identical, so pilots could easily qualify to fly both.

The Airbus A320 family are narrow-body airliners launched in March 1984 and first flown on February 22, 1987, and introduced in April 1988 by Air France. The A320 carries 180 passengers. It was the first airliner to feature an "envelope of safety," preventing pilots from making unsafe maneuvers.

WIDE BODY "JUMBO" JETS

Wide body jets have two aisles, and have a longer range.

The Boeing 747 is a large, long-range wide-body airliner. It first flew in 1969. Pan Am wanted a wide plane to fit more people so that tickets could be cheaper, democratizing air travel. The 747 was the first airplane dubbed a "jumbo jet," the first wide-body airliner. It could carry 366 passengers. The military and NASA also used it. It is pictured here carrying the space shuttle orbiter.

The DC-10 is a wide body, long range, tri-jet. It first flew on February 25, 1965. It carries 285 passengers and has a range of 4,800 miles.

The Boeing 767 is a twin-engine, wide-body jet first produced in 1978. The B-767 was developed concurrently with the 757, so both shared the same technological advances in aerodynamics, avionics, and materials. The pioneering two-crew computerized flight decks, or "glass cockpits," of the 757 and 767 are nearly identical, so pilots can easily qualify to fly both. It seats 200 passengers and has a range of 3,900 miles.

The Airbus A380-800 is a passenger plane made in France with capacity for 853 passengers in a single class or 644 in a two-tiered class. It has a travel range of 8,208 miles.

The Boeing 777 is the largest twin jet; it first flew in 1994. It has an envelope of safety, similar to Airbus. It can carry up to 368 passengers.

Connect with Mary: shipkobush@gmail.com

Did I miss you? Would you like to be included in an update of the book? If so, please contact me. When I have a second edition, I will add your information.

BIBLIOGRAPHY

Books:

Cooper, Ann Lewis. *Weaving the Winds, Emily Howell Warner*. Bloomington, Indiana: 1st Book Library, Bloomington, 2003.

Friedan, Betty. *Feminine Mystique: The Classic that Sparked a Feminist Revolution*. W.W. Norton & Company, Reprint 2001.

O'Neill, Norah. *Flying Tigress: A Memoir*. Ascending Journey Press, 2005.

Shipko, Mary Bush. *Aviatrix: First Woman Pilot for Hughes Airwest*. CreateSpace, 2015.

Thomas, Gillian. *Because of Sex: One Law, Ten Cases, and Fifty Years that Changed American Women's Lives at Work*. St. Martin Press, 2016.

Tiburzi, Bonnie, and Moolman, Valerie. *Takeoff.* New York, New York: Eleanor Friede/Crown Publishers, Inc., 1984.

Turner Publishing. *The Ninety-Nines: Yesterday-Today-Tomorrow*, 1996.

Welch, Rosanne. *Encyclopedia of Women in Aviation and Space*. Santa Barbara, Calif: ABC-CLIO, 1998.

Magazine, Newspaper, and Internet Articles:

Adams, Matt. "Meet our first African American woman pilot." *United Hub*, February 26, 2018. Retrieved from https://hub.united.com/united-african-american-woman-pilot-2540113430.html.

Ahn, Sam, and Lydia Jakub. "Advancing Women in Aviation." *Air Line Pilots Association, Int'l (ALPA)*. Retrieved from https://www.alpa.org/news-and-events/air-line-pilot-magazine/advancing-women-in-aviation.

Albrecht, Brian. "Delta Airlines' first black woman pilot, a Cleveland native, comes home to share passion for aviation." *AP News*, January 22, 2018. Retrieved from https://apnews.com/article/ohio-cleveland-archive-race-and-ethnicity-1a008dba05a94285b3c7305d685dccce.

Aviation Camps of the Carolinas. "The first African-American female pilot in US Navy history." http://www.aviationcamps.org/meetbrenda.html.

Beresnevicius, Rytis. "Automation in the Aviation Industry – The Future Is Automated." *Aerotime Hub*. Retrieved from https://www.aerotime.aero/23162-automation-aviation-industry.

Bethea, Leah S. "Pilot who makes her home in Milledgeville paying it forward for other women." *Union-Recorder*, March 24, 2022. Retrieved from https://www.unionrecorder.com/news/pilot-who-makes-her-home-in-milledgeville-paying-it-forward-for-other-women/article_b0ab6034-abb1-11ec-8ca9-b7d8ac4548b3.html.

Cook, Dawn. "Presenter Biography." National Training Aircraft Symposium, 2017.

Fortier, Rénald. "Turi Widerøe paid a flying visit to Montréal the other day." *Ingenium Channel*, March

9, 2020. Retrieved from https://ingeniumcanada.
org/channel/articles/turi-wideroe-paid-a-flying-visi
t-to-montreal-the-other-day.

Fuji, Ari. "Japanese Aviator."

Goh, Brenda. "In China, female pilots strain to hold up half
the sky." *Reuters*, November 5, 2018.

Gorny, Nicki. "Sky's the limit for pilot, author: Local
pioneer helped smooth the way for today's female
pilots." *The Toledo Blade*, July 15, 2018.

Hamilton, Sherry. "Mary Shipko's life in the skies began at
an early age." *Gazette-Journal*, April 22, 2021.

Horne, Thomas A. "A Fly-By-Wire Future? Digital
Flight Controls, on the March." *AOPA Foundation*,
October 1, 2020. Retrieved from https://www.
aopa.org/news-and-media/all-news/2020/october/
pilot/a-fly-by-wire-future.

Hyess, Mbeti. "The Flying Scholar. How many careers can
one woman have? Abigail Davis '72 would answer: As
many as she wants." *Ithaca Aluminaries*, last updated
June 1, 2006.

IATA. "Advancing Gender Balance by 2025." Retrieved
from https://www.iata.org/en/policy/future-o
f-airlines-2035/25-by-2025/.

Ige, Tofarati. "I'm happy not sacrificing my family for
career—Chinyere Kalu." *Punch*. Retrieved from
https://punchng.com/im-happy-not-sacrificing-my-fa
mily-for-career-chinyere-kalu/.

Koigi, Bob. "[Kenya] Irene Koki's towering career as first
female African Dreamliner Captain." *Africa Business
Communities*, 24-01-2020. Retrieved from https://
africabusinesscommunities.com/news/kenya-iren

e-kokis-towering-career-as-first-female-african-dr
eamliner-captain/.

Kraus, Theresa L. "The CAA Helps America Prepare for
World War II." Retrieved from https://www.faa.gov/
about/history/milestones/media/The_CAA_Helps_
America_Prepare_for_World_WarII.pdf.

Lakritz, Talia. "13 groundbreaking female pilots throughout
history who shattered the glass ceiling." *Business Insider
India*, June 13, 2020.

McGraw, Eliza. "This Ace Aviatrix Learned to Fly
Even Though Orville Wright Refused to Teach Her."
Smithsonianmag.com, March 22, 2017.

National Aviation Hall of Fame. "Warner, Emily Howell."
https://www.nationalaviation.org/our-enshrinees/
warner-emily-howell/.

Nixon, Stuart. "First Ladies of the Flight Deck." *Air Line
Pilot*, May 1978.

Russian Aviation. "Elena Novichkova—first female A320
captain for Aeroflot." Ruaviation.com.

Ruttenber, Jessica. "An Open Letter to the Women of
Firsts." *Hidden Barriers* (blog). https://hidden-barriers.
org/2021/01/15/an-open-letter-to-the-women-of-firsts/.

Salam, Afia. "The Sky Is the Limit."

Shekhar, Shashank. "First Indian woman to
command jet engine aircraft retires." *The
Indian Express*, April 1, 2010. http://archive.
indianexpress.com/news/first-indian-woman-t
o-command-jet-engine-aircraft-retires/598384/.

Sit, Jane, and Yoko Wakatsuki. "Meet Japan's first female
commercial airline captain." *CNN Travel*, May 6, 2019.

Tedeschi, Diane. "Fly Girls." *Air & Space*. Retrieved from https://www.airspacemag.com/history-of-flight/fly-girls-180970903/.

Wikipedia. "Women Airforce Service Pilots." https://en.wikipedia.org/wiki/Women_Airforce_Service_Pilots.

Ying, Cheryl, and Vernette Didier Chia. "From accountant to female pilot." Retrieved from https://www.tnp.sg/news/singapore-news/accountant-female-pilot.

https://www.eaa.org/eaa

https://isa21.org/

https://www.wai.org